THE
AMERICAN
STYLE

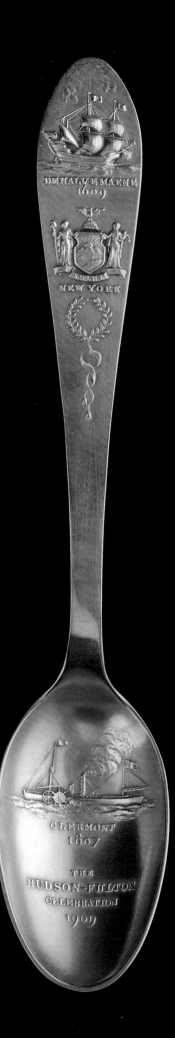

THE
AMERICAN
STYLE

COLONIAL
REVIVAL
AND THE
MODERN
METROPOLIS

Donald Albrecht
Thomas Mellins

MUSEUM OF THE CITY OF NEW YORK
THE MONACELLI PRESS

This book and the exhibition it accompanies are made possible, in part,
by generous grants from the following:

Taconic Builders
Jenny and John Paulson
The Bodman Foundation
Benjamin Moore & Co.
Jamie Drake
Gerry Charitable Trust
Robert A. M. Stern Architects, LLP
Elisha-Bolton Foundation
Furthermore: A Program of the J. M. Kaplan Fund
Graham Foundation for Advanced Studies in the Fine Arts
New York State Council on the Arts
New York Design Center—James P. Druckman
The Felicia Fund, Inc.
Mottahedeh & Company
Gil Schafer III
The Roy J. Zuckerberg Family Foundation, on behalf of Lloyd P. Zuckerberg
Lee Gelber
Richard H. Jenrette
Janet C. Ross
Janet Schlesinger

Published in the United States by The Monacelli Press, a division of Random House, Inc., New York.

The Monacelli Press and M logo are trademarks of Random House, Inc.

Library of Congress Cataloging-in-Publication Data

Albrecht, Donald.
The American style : Colonial Revival in New York City / Donald Albrecht, Thomas Mellins. -- 1st ed.
p. cm.
Issued in connection with an exhibition held June 7 through Nov 6, 2011, at the Museum of the City of
New York.
Includes bibliographical references and index.
ISBN 978-1-58093-285-1 (hardcover : alk. paper)
1. Architecture, Domestic--New York (State)--New York. 2. Colonial revival (Architecture)--New York
(State)--New York. 3. Architecture and society--New York (State)--New York--History--20th century.
4. Decorative arts, Early American--Influence. I. Mellins, Thomas. II. Museum of the City of New York.
III. Title. IV. Title: Colonial Revival in New York City.
NA7238.N6A43 2011
720.9747´109041--dc22

2010050478

Printed in China

10 9 8 7 6 5 4 3 2 1
First edition

Design: Abbott Miller, Kristen Spilman, Pentagram

www.monacellipress.com

Captions:
Page 2: Silver sugar bowl manufactured by Tiffany & Co., 1915–19.
Page 3: Commemorative spoon from Hudson-Fulton Celebration, Tiffany & Co., 1909.
Page 4: Silver tray manufactured by Tiffany & Co., 1915–19.
Page 5: Gold salver manufactured by Starr & Frost-Gorham, Inc., 1936.
Page 6: Gold coffeepot manufactured by Starr & Frost-Gorham, Inc., 1936.
Page 10: Doorway of Susan Wagner Wing, Gracie Mansion, New York City, 1966.
Photograph by Cervin Robinson, 1990.

CONTENTS

« 11 »

PREFACE
Susan Henshaw Jones

« 13 »

WHAT IS
COLONIAL REVIVAL?

« 34 »

A FLEXIBLE GRAMMAR:
ARCHITECTURE AND
INTERIOR DESIGN

« 166 »

COLONIAL BIBLES
AND BALLYHOO: PUBLICATIONS,
EXHIBITIONS, AND STAGE-SET
ARCHITECTURE

« 114 »

COLONIAL CHIC:
DECORATIVE ARTS

« 198 »

EPILOGUE
AN ENDURING STYLE:
COLONIAL REVIVAL TODAY

« 220 »

NOTES

« 223 »

BOARD OF TRUSTEES

« 222 »

ACKNOWLEDGMENTS

« 224 »

PHOTOGRAPHY SOURCES

PREFACE

IN 1932, WHEN THE NINE-YEAR-OLD MUSEUM OF THE CITY OF New York moved into its home at Fifth Avenue and 104th Street, Manhattan was already internationally celebrated as a skyscraper city. Yet, while New York City was synonymous with modernity, many New Yorkers were looking back and evaluating anew the "traditional" styles embodied in American Colonial architecture and design. The Museum's stately red-brick structure, designed by Joseph H. Freedlander, was a key component of New York's contribution to a nationwide Colonial Revival. This book and the exhibition it accompanies use the Museum's own building as a starting point for the exploration of this important, but sometimes over-looked, movement. In twentieth-century New York and its suburbs, archi-tectural highlights included buildings by Delano & Aldrich and Mott B. Schmidt and suburban enclaves in the Bronx by Dwight James Baum and on Long Island by builder José M. Allegue. Very importantly, the move-ment also produced a wide array of furniture, like the excellent pieces made by Master Craftsmen, and decorative home elements, from tea services by Tiffany & Co. to crystal candlesticks by Steuben Glass. But, as this project reveals, the Colonial Revival is more than nostalgia for the past: the refined architectural style developed during the country's early years is a living vocabulary that is perpetually rediscovered and re-invented.

The able curators who shaped the content of the exhibition and book are Donald Albrecht, the Museum's curator of architecture and design, and Thomas Mellins. The exhibition's designer is Peter Pennoyer of Peter Pennoyer Architects, and Abbott Miller of Pentagram designed this book and the exhibition's graphics. Susan Gail Johnson very capably provided assistance.

This book and its companion exhibition were made possible by lead support from Taconic Builders, whose founding partner James E. Hanley is both a co-chair of this project and a Museum trustee. Serving with him as co-chairs are James P. Druckman, of the New York Design Center, Jamie Drake, and Stephen S. Lash, and I thank them for championing this project and convincing others to support the Museum's work. Grants from the Gerry Charitable Trust; the Graham Foundation for Advanced Studies in the Fine Arts; Furthermore: A Program of the J.M. Kaplan Fund; and the New York State Council on the Arts, a state agency, supported this publication. And, I am grateful to Jenny and John Paulson; The Bodman Foundation; Benjamin Moore & Co.; Robert A. M. Stern Architects, LLP; the New York Design Center; the Elisha-Bolton Foundation; The Felicia Fund, Inc.; Mottahedeh & Company; Gil Schafer III; The Roy J. Zuckerberg Family Foundation, on behalf of Lloyd P. Zuckerberg; Lee Gelber; Richard H. Jenrette; Janet C. Ross; and Janet Schlesinger. In-kind support was provided by Benjamin Moore & Co. and *The Magazine Antiques*.

Finally, the Museum is very pleased to work with the Institute for Classical Architecture & Classical America as co-sponsors.

Susan Henshaw Jones
Ronay Menschel Director
Museum of the City of New York

WHAT IS COLONIAL REVIVAL?

COLONIAL REVIVAL ARCHITECTURE IS INSTANTLY RECOGNIZABLE: red brick, white-painted clapboard, shingled siding, columned porches, multipaned windows with shutters, paneled wood doors framed by rectangular sidelights and topped by leaded fanlights. In the realm of decoration, the Colonial Revival looks back to silver tea services, scenic wallpapers, and furniture made by Duncan Phyfe and other master cabinetmakers in traditional materials such as mahogany. Above all, the Colonial Revival style is defined by its attention to proportion and an overall sense of elegance derived from economy and restraint.

Throughout its history and continuing today, the Colonial Revival has been used to invoke a national experience and express national values. In the process of celebrating aspects of early America, architects, designers, and promoters have refined and popularized a particular look, but they have also constructed an invented past. This portrait of the nation's origins is more evocative than precise. It has often been stripped of history's grittier aspects, and as a result has offered a sense of comfort and elegant simplicity that many have found reassuring, particularly in times of radical change. For those with long family histories in America, the Colonial Revival style expresses a sense of authority and pride; it has also been used as a tool for inculcating more recent arrivals with American tastes and a sense of belonging. Yet the relationship between the Colonial Revival and change has been complex, at times taking on a xenophobic dimension.

Despite its signature appearance and cultural significance, however, the definition and the stylistic sources of the Colonial Revival are difficult to pinpoint. Strictly speaking, the term applies to the period bookended by the establishment of Jamestown, Virginia, in 1607, and the Revolutionary War. The term is most commonly associated with New England's Georgian architecture, named for the monarchs who ruled Britain and its colonies beginning in 1714. But by the end of the

CENTURY VASE DESIGNED BY KARL L. H. MÜLLER, C. 1876.

Commemorating the nation's centennial, this vase designed by the sculptor Karl L. H. Müller and manufactured by the Union Porcelain Works in Brooklyn, New York, incorporated imagery drawn from American history. It was based on a series of larger works also by Müller that had been shown at the Union Porcelain Works display at the 1876 Centennial Exhibition in Philadelphia.

nineteenth century, Colonial Revival had come to refer to more far-ranging sources. These include Cape Cod "saltbox" cottages and Dutch Colonial houses, as well as the architecture and design of the early Republic, known as the Federal style; the term "Colonial Revival" has even been stretched to encompass so-called "Southern Colonial" houses inspired by columned ante-bellum mansions.[1] In fact, any architecture built after the founding of the country that looked backward to earlier American precedents has been considered Colonial Revival. The architectural historian Richard Guy Wilson, for example, argues that the iconic steeple of Philadelphia's Independence Hall, which was added in 1828—more than fifty years after the completion of the building—is an example of the Colonial Revival.[2] That this addition came so closely on the heels of the Colonial period itself raises the question: is the Colonial Revival indeed a revival, or is it a part of an ongoing, living vocabulary?

This book—and the exhibition it accompanies—contends that while the forms and materials of American Colonial architecture and design have been consistently and creatively mined for more than two centuries, many of the most robust and inventive manifestations of the style were created between 1876 and the end of the 1930s. This period of creativity was sparked by the centennial, when Americans' interest in their past was reawakened as a result of both nostalgia for a seemingly simpler past without modern technologies and booming cities whose growth was spurred by immigration, and satisfaction in how far the nation had progressed since its founding. This heyday culminated in the boom-and-bust decades of the 1920s and 1930s, with high-style architects and designers garnering the support of a network of collectors, curators, and merchants.

A major watershed in the evolution of the Colonial Revival occurred in 1877 when four young architects—Charles Follen McKim, William Rutherford Mead, William Bigelow, and Stanford White—toured New England, sketching and measuring historic Colonial-era houses in Marblehead, Newburyport, and Salem, Massachusetts, as well as in Portsmouth, New Hampshire. Even before this joint effort, McKim had visited and sketched Colonial-era buildings for years on his own in Newport, Rhode Island. In the process, a new direction in American architecture was forged. The firm of McKim, Mead & White was established in New York in 1879, and three years later the architects began to design the H. A. C. Taylor House in Newport. Completed in 1886, the house was a pioneering example of the Colonial Revival. McKim, Mead & White, which worked in a range of classically inspired styles, followed its earliest foray in the Colonial Revival with the Mount Vernon–inspired James L. Breese House (1906) on Long Island, as well as numerous residences in New York City.

H. A. C. TAYLOR HOUSE, NEWPORT, RHODE ISLAND, MCKIM, MEAD & WHITE, 1882–86, AS SEEN IN THE FIRM'S MONOGRAPH.

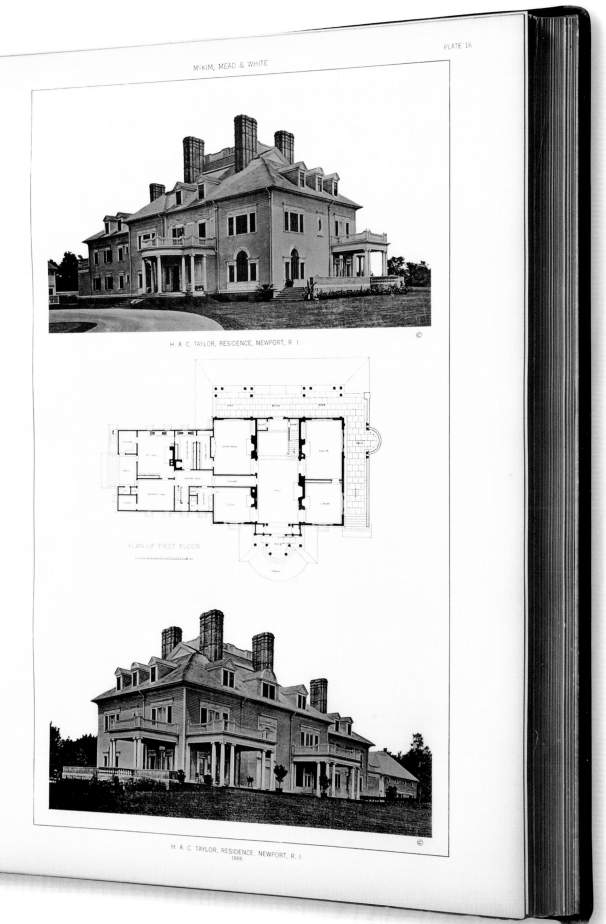

PLATE 16

McKIM, MEAD & WHITE

H. A. C. TAYLOR, RESIDENCE, NEWPORT, R. I.

PLAN OF FIRST FLOOR

H. A. C. TAYLOR, RESIDENCE, NEWPORT, R. I.
1886

JAMES L. BREESE HOUSE, SOUTHAMPTON, NEW YORK, MCKIM, MEAD & WHITE, 1906.
PHOTOGRAPH BY JONATHAN WALLEN, 1997.

HILL-STEAD, FARMINGTON, CONNECTICUT, THEODATE POPE RIDDLE, 1901.
PHOTOGRAPH BY JERRY L. THOMPSON, 2005.

Working with Edgerton Swartout, a young architect in the firm of McKim, Mead &
White, Theodate Pope Riddle was principally responsible for the design of this house,
which she shared with her parents. Hill-Stead looked to Mount Vernon for inspiration,
but it also represented Riddle's personal interpretation of the ideal farmhouse.
The design combines features such as bay windows and the latest mechanical
conveniences with Mount Vernon's imposing colonnaded porch.

RENDERING OF MASSACHUSETTS STATE BUILDING, WORLD'S COLUMBIAN EXPOSITION,
CHICAGO, PEABODY AND STEARNS, 1893.

PRIVATE AND CONFIDENTIAL, A HAND-TINTED
PHOTOGRAPH BY WALLACE NUTTING ART PRINTS STUDIO, C. 1910.

PEMBROKE ROOM (OR PINE KITCHEN), BEAUPORT, GLOUCESTER, MASSACHUSETTS,
HENRY DAVIS SLEEPER, BEGUN IN 1917.
PHOTOGRAPH BY DAVID BOHL, 1990.

STEREOPTICON OF THE PINE ROOM, WINTERTHUR, DELAWARE, 1935.

STUDY, CHESTERTOWN, SOUTHAMPTON, NEW YORK,
CROSS & CROSS WITH INTERIORS BY HENRY DAVIS SLEEPER, 1925.

FOYER, CHESTERTOWN.

DINING ROOM, CHESTERTOWN.

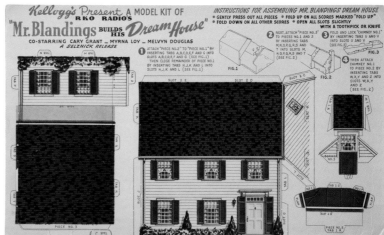

HOUSE MODEL KIT BASED ON THE MOVIE
MR. BLANDINGS BUILDS HIS DREAM HOUSE, C.1948.

This Blandings Dream House Kit was one of a series created by Kellogg's. Available through
the mail, the how-to kits were promoted on the company's cereal boxes.

Between the centennial and World War II, the Colonial Revival
was a national phenomenon applied to a broad range of building types
and practiced by many leading architects. These included David Adler,
William Lawrence Bottomley, Delano & Aldrich, Wilson Eyre, Charles
Platt, John Russell Pope, Theodate Pope Riddle, James Gamble
Rogers, John F. Staub, and Hobart Upjohn. In addition to buildings
that synthesized Colonial forms with contemporary building programs—
residences, schools, and civic buildings—temporary structures were
inspired by actual Colonial buildings, such as Peabody and Stearns's
Massachusetts State Building at the 1893 Chicago World's Columbian
Exposition, modeled after the John Hancock House (1740) in Boston.

Outside the architectural profession, three individuals, Wallace
Nutting, Henry Francis du Pont, and John D. Rockefeller Jr., can be
singled out for playing seminal roles in advancing the Colonial Revival on
a national scale. Nutting, a minister turned Colonial Revival propagandist,
summed up his philosophy as "Not all the old is good but all the new is
bad."[3] Nutting starting taking photographs of the American countryside
around 1900, and in 1904 he opened the Wallace Nutting Art Prints
Studio in New York, where he sold the images. For nearly three decades,
Nutting, who moved to Connecticut in 1906, pursued numerous Colonial
Revival projects. He bought Colonial houses and opened them to tourists.
He staged and photographed period-appropriate tableaux inside his
houses, employed hundreds of colorists to hand paint the photographs,
and sold them nationwide as decorative accents. Beginning in 1917,
Nutting fabricated reproductions of seventeenth- and eighteenth-century

POSTCARD OF COLONIAL
WILLIAMSBURG.

COLONIAL WILLIAMSBURG
BROCHURE, C.1937.

American furniture. He also wrote extensively about his passion; his 1928 two-volume book *Furniture Treasury*, with five thousand photographs taken by him, is still considered an invaluable pictorial guide to the furniture of the nation's early years.

Perhaps the era's greatest collector of Americana was Henry Francis du Pont, whose two homes, Chestertown and Winterthur, were the focus of his efforts. In 1924 du Pont commissioned the New York architecture firm Cross & Cross to design a fifty-room house, called Chestertown in Southampton, Long Island. The interiors featured paneling, woodwork, and architectural elements from different eighteenth-century houses; most came from the Maryland town of Chestertown, which gave the house its name. Chestertown's re-created interiors fit into a Colonial Revival tradition of so-called "period rooms" that sought to show visitors how early Americans lived. Among the earliest exemplars were the Colonial-era kitchens and bedrooms created from the end of the nineteenth century by Charles P. Wilcomb in public institutions in San Francisco and Oakland, as well as Pittsburgh.

To create Chestertown's interiors, du Pont turned to the designer Henry Davis Sleeper. Sleeper promoted Colonial Revival to a socially prominent clientele on Boston's North Shore, and du Pont admired Beauport, his summer house in Gloucester, Massachusetts. This house was an encyclopedia of early American architectural elements and decorative objects. "Mightn't it be fun," Sleeper asked, "to have a house in which each room could recapture some of the spirit of a specific mood or phase or 'period' of our American life from the time of Plymouth down through the revolution or early Republic?"[4] Sleeper's favorite room was a New England style Colonial kitchen. He named it the "Pembroke Room" after the town in Massachusetts where Robert Barker, an ancestor, had built a saltbox cottage in 1650, and where seven generations of his family had subsequently lived for more than two hundred years.

After working with Sleeper on Chestertown, du Pont turned his efforts to Winterthur, a far grander estate outside Wilmington, Delaware, which featured some of the country's most elaborate period rooms, including a Colonial kitchen inspired by Sleeper's Pembroke Room. The du Pont family had purchased the estate in the early nineteenth century, but the property's status as a museum began in earnest when Henry inherited it in 1927, shortly after the completion of Chestertown. In 1930 du Pont established the nonprofit, educational Winterthur Corporation with the express purpose of transforming his home into a museum devoted to early American decorative arts. By 1932 du Pont had doubled the size of the building to accommodate his collections, and in 1951 he opened the house-museum to the public.

While Beauport, Chestertown, and Winterthur preserved elements of America's Colonial past, the preservation and reconstruction of an entire town was achieved at Colonial Williamsburg in Virginia. Encouraged by W. A. R. Goodwin, rector of Williamsburg's Bruton Parish Church, and aided by a team of consultants, John D. Rockefeller Jr. financed the restoration and reconstruction of the former Colonial capital. The project began in 1926 and opened to the public in stages throughout the 1930s. Nearly 600 post-Colonial buildings on the site were demolished, while 188 Colonial structures were rebuilt on their original foundations and 88 were restored.

Colonial Williamsburg's ongoing role as a tourist destination has been accompanied by the sale of period wallpapers, furniture, and lines of paint colors that remain popular today. While the accuracy of the restoration has long been challenged, Colonial Williamsburg, in its aura of a genteel America formed in the Depression, sheds light on why this expressive style endures. The Colonial Revival is an American style, fulfilling a collective desire for tradition, while offering a malleable sense of the past, shaped by ever-changing contemporary forces.

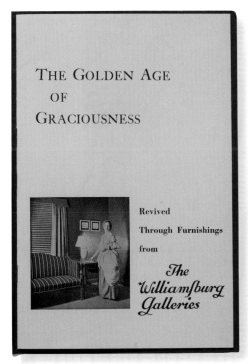
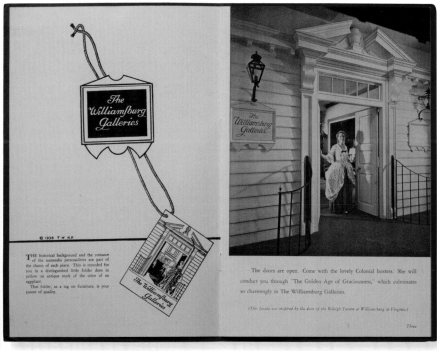

BROCHURE FOR THE WILLIAMSBURG GALLERIES, C. 1936.

Beginning in 1936, a company called Williamsburg Craftsmen created reproduction furnishings approved by Colonial Williamsburg. They were sold in architectural settings that recreated the Colonial capital's Raleigh Tavern. Williamsburg Galleries were built in leading department stores nationwide, from Jordan Marsh in Boston to Marshall Field's in Chicago and Bullock's in Los Angeles.

COLONIAL REVIVAL AND NEW YORK CITY

New York City—the ultimate modern metropolis, filled with new arrivals, endlessly changing and rebuilding itself in a heedless rush to the future—would seem unlikely ground for anything evoking the past. Yet, surprisingly, this most up-to-date city and its environs have long been home to some of the world's great revivalist styles of architecture and design. None has been more enduring than the Colonial Revival. New York–based architects and designers created superb examples of the style. It was, however, the formation of a network of museums, publishers, and department stores that developed and disseminated the style that made New York's contribution unique.

New York City's interest in its own Colonial past came early. In 1831, more than twenty years before the rescue of a then-neglected Mount Vernon brought national attention to architectural preservation, the editors of the *New-York Mirror* protested the demolition of a Dutch Colonial house located in lower Manhattan, arguing that the event was "in compliance with that irreverence for antiquity which so grievously afflicts the people of this city."[5] By the end of the nineteenth century, as parts of the city were being radically transformed into a modern metropolis of skyscrapers, subways, and tenements, historic preservation took on new urgency. In 1897 the Van Cortlandt Mansion (1748) in the Bronx became the first of the city's Colonial house-museums; twenty years later, a Colonial herb garden was created on the house's property. By 1915 Fraunces Tavern (1719), the Morris-Jumel Mansion (1765), the Dyckman House (c. 1783), and the Poe Cottage (c. 1812) had all been preserved and opened to the public.[6]

When it came to new construction, the style's formal qualities—flat facades, shallow ornamentation, and rectangular spaces—made the Colonial Revival an ideal urban style well suited to New York City's density. While the style connected the city to its past, Colonial forms were freely adapted to the contemporary programs of building types unimagined by the nation's early settlers, and realized at the metropolitan scale of New York City. The style was, in fact, comprised of a wide range of vocabularies, from strict interpretations of historical models to freer adaptations that utilized new materials and means of construction and manufacturing. Even today, after decades of change and redevelopment, the city is filled with distinguished Colonial Revival buildings by well-known firms such as McKim, Mead & White and lesser-known practitioners including Mott B. Schmidt and Dwight James Baum.

After World War I, as car ownership became increasingly common, many New Yorkers moved from dense residential neighborhoods to suburban-style developments in Queens, the Bronx, and outlying areas. The Colonial Revival style, which has strong associations with freestanding single-family houses, became a standard

116 EAST 55TH ST. NEW YORK.

WILLIAM ZIEGLER HOUSE, EAST 55TH STREET BETWEEN PARK AND LEXINGTON AVENUES,
NEW YORK CITY, WILLIAM LAWRENCE BOTTOMLEY, 1927.
PHOTOGRAPH BY WURTS BROTHERS COMPANY.

STREETSCAPE OF OLDER BROWNSTONES AND NEWER COLONIAL REVIVAL TOWNHOUSES, 122–130 EAST 89TH STREET, NEW YORK CITY, C. 1911.

Described by Edith Wharton in her 1934 memoir *A Backward Glance* as "the most hideous stone ever quarried," brownstone, a favorite material of the nineteenth century, was often replaced in the early twentieth century with stucco or brick facades in various styles, including Colonial Revival. The renovated houses, their stoops removed, often extended forward to their property lines.

ADVERTISEMENT FOR DEVELOPMENT OF JAMAICA PARK SOUTH, QUEENS, NEW YORK, 1908.

feature of new residential developments. The style was also applied to apartment buildings, public buildings, and shopping centers, adding an instant sense of history for an increasingly transient population. While many new suburbanites commuted daily to Art Deco skyscraper office buildings in Manhattan, the Colonial Revival style offered a reassuringly familiar sense of home and community. Additionally, it was considered a sound investment. "Styles in homes come and go like styles in cars," the editors of *Popular Mechanics* noted in 1929. "It pays to build in a style as liquid in public approval as a Liberty bond at the bank. Colonial is such a style."[7]

New York was also home to Colonial Revival authors, scholars, and merchants, who precipitated two key shifts in the nation's embrace of the style. First, while until the end of the nineteenth century Colonial and Federal buildings and artifacts were valued for their associations with historical figures—"the George Washington slept here" phenomenon— New Yorkers brought a heightened level of connoisseurship to American decorative arts. Second, in the 1920s, a group of influential tastemakers propelled New York City, by then the epicenter of American finance and fashion, into becoming the nation's antiques capital.

MAURICE GREENBERG HOUSE, HEWLETT BAY PARK, NEW YORK,
MORTIMER FREEHOF / JOHN FINN, 1948.
PHOTOGRAPH BY KAREN A. DOMBROVSKI-SOBEL, 2001.

opposite

GARDNER B. PERRY HOUSE, 146 WHITESTONE AVENUE, FLUSHING, QUEENS,
NEW YORK, HOBART UPJOHN, 1929.
PHOTOGRAPH BY SAMUEL H. GOTTSCHO.

VESTIBULE, GARDNER B. PERRY HOUSE.
PHOTOGRAPH BY SAMUEL H. GOTTSCHO.

BEDROOM, GARDNER B. PERRRY HOUSE.
PHOTOGRAPH BY SAMUEL H. GOTTSCHO.

The opening in 1924 of the Metropolitan Museum of Art's American Wing, primarily comprised of period rooms, marked a key moment in both of these transitions. The American Wing was, in fact, part of a larger tradition at the museum. In 1909, for example, curator and collector R. T. Haines Halsey, later curator of the American Wing, assembled furniture attributed to the workshop of accomplished early American cabinetmakers for the museum's *Hudson-Fulton Exhibition of American Industrial Arts*. This show elevated American decorative arts by presenting them, for the first time in a major exhibition, alongside the nation's paintings and sculpture. Halsey's efforts were supplemented by those of others in the 1920s, such as entrepreneur, designer, and antiques expert Nancy Vincent McClelland; businessman and collector Louis Guerineau Myers; dealer and furniture maker Jacob Margolis, who moved to New York from Hartford; Boston collector and dealer Israel Sack, who opened a shop in Manhattan around 1927; and *The Magazine Antiques*,

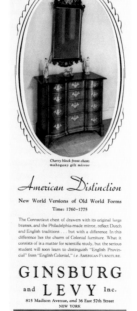

THE KNICKERBOCKER KITCHEN, BROOKLYN SANITARY FAIR, 1864.
CHROMOLITHOGRAPH BY A. BROWN & CO.

ADVERTISEMENT FOR ISRAEL SACK, INC.,
THE MAGAZINE ANTIQUES, FEBRUARY 1940.

ADVERTISEMENT FOR GINSBURG AND LEVY, INC.,
THE MAGAZINE ANTIQUES, APRIL 1940.

which by 1930 had moved its office to New York from Boston. And, when Wallace Nutting wanted to increase sales in the early 1920s, he turned to that most modern of modern endeavors—advertising—and hired New York's George Batten Company (later Batten, Barton, Durstine, and Osborn, or BBDO) to place advertisements in periodicals from *Vogue* to *Good Housekeeping*.

New Yorkers also advanced the Colonial Revival through elaborate public events, staged during moments of both celebration, such as the Hudson-Fulton Celebration of 1909, and adversity, from war to economic depression. Colonial-inspired events can be traced back to the Civil War, when New York women, working with the United States Sanitary Commission (a forerunner of the American Red Cross), aided the war effort by hosting re-creations of "old-time" kitchens at large-scale fairs. (These kitchens were informal precursors to the period rooms of Winterthur and the Metropolitan Museum.) Against the backdrop of a nation at war with itself, the so-called "Knickerbocker Kitchen" in Manhattan and "New England Kitchen" in Brooklyn were used to evoke an earlier time defined by domestic tranquility and national unity. To give the Manhattan display an aura of authenticity, objects were sought from people's homes through the *New York Times*. In April 1864, the *Times* reported that "'ransacking' became the order of the day among the descendants of the Knickerbockers. There was poking about in dusty garrets, there was rummaging in ancient chests and antiquated bureaus, there was a general overhauling of long forgotten lumber, and from all the litter and dust, from neglected nooks and crannies, piece by piece, the relics of the seventeenth century emerged, and the fullest and most valuable collection of venerable antiques ever got together [was] placed in the hands of the committee."[8]

In 1932, at the depths of the Great Depression, the nation's legacy of Colonial-era architecture and decorative arts was once again used to symbolize national unity and triumph over adversity. Coming three years after the stock market crash, with unemployment high in New York and Hoovervilles filling the streets and Central Park, the bicentennial of Washington's birth was accompanied by celebrations centered on full-scale reconstructions of Federal Hall in Manhattan's Bryant Park and Mount Vernon in Brooklyn's Prospect Park. Referring to the 1932 event, Eleanor Roosevelt, then First Lady of New York State, asserted that it was "good for all of us in the trying times we are going through to consider those early days, when the problems were probably even greater, and learn the lessons which the characters of the men who founded the United States have to teach us."[9]

Seven years later, the era of "trying times" and uncertainty continued to hold sway as the United States still endured economic hardship, now combined with the threat of war. The New York World's Fair of 1939/40, though best known for its streamlined pavilions and displays of wondrous appliances, also featured a "Town of Tomorrow" which, curiously, included many traditional homes, amid modern ones, in an idyllic suburban enclave. This mix expressed the architectural culture

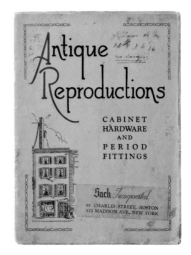

ANTIQUE REPRODUCTIONS BROCHURE FOR ISRAEL SACK, INC., 1950S.

While Sack is best known as a collector and dealer, he also sold reproductions of Colonial architectural hardware.

of the time, which had proven fertile ground for a multiplicity of aesthetic vocabularies. Out of this context, a so-called "battle of the styles" emerged, which after World War II gave way to an architectural scene dominated by a minimalist Modernism of steel-and-glass structures. At least in the eyes of most progressive architects and critics, historicist styles were relegated to the sidelines.

Nonetheless, there were still-vibrant masters of the Colonial Revival style active on the contemporary scene, such as Mott B. Schmidt, who had been celebrated for his interwar residences. In 1965 Schmidt designed an addition to Gracie Mansion, New York City's official mayoral residence; the addition, which became known as the Susan Wagner Wing, in honor of Mayor Robert Wagner's late wife, was completed in 1966. *New York Times* architecture critic Ada Louise Huxtable, who championed modern architecture, gave the building a mixed review. Having described an earlier proposal by a different architect as possessing "all the charm of a suburban garage," Huxtable noted that while the addition "makes it clear that the 18th century, with its virtually irreproducible architectural details . . . and its top-of-the-market antiques, is only for the very rich and nostalgic," Schmidt's work nonetheless was "impeccably executed" and "superbly appointed."[10]

For some younger members of the architectural profession, however, Schmidt's essay in the Colonial Revival went far beyond that appeal to encompass broader lessons for the future of American architectural practice. Robert A. M. Stern, then a New York architect fresh out of Yale, had initially "reviled" the building, but found it "a revelation" upon visiting it. "Looking at what Schmidt could accomplish with such style in a language then deemed 'dead' by most architects," Stern later wrote from a twenty-five-year vantage point, "I began to see new possibilities."[11] For Stern, as for other architects, as well as interior decorators and designers, a new chapter had opened on the future of an enduring American style.

RECONSTRUCTION OF FEDERAL HALL IN BRYANT PARK FOR THE BICENTENNIAL OF GEORGE WASHINGTON'S BIRTH, NEW YORK CITY, JOSEPH H. FREEDLANDER, 1932.

RENDERING OF THE WEST ELEVATION OF GRACIE MANSION, SHOWING SUSAN WAGNER WING
ON RIGHT, CARL SCHURZ PARK BETWEEN EAST 88TH AND 89TH STREETS, NEW YORK CITY,
MOTT B. SCHMIDT, 1965.

DOORWAY OF SUSAN WAGNER WING.
PHOTOGRAPH BY CERVIN ROBINSON, 1990.

I am a strong believer in tradition but tradition tempered with motion.

— WILLIAM ADAMS DELANO, 1940

A FLEXIBLE GRAMMAR

ARCHITECTURE AND INTERIOR DESIGN

RESIDENCES

MCKIM, MEAD & WHITE

In 1911 the editors of *Architecture* magazine, in their assessment of
a trend away from America's exclusive reliance on European models,
singled out the firm of McKim, Mead & White for its pioneering efforts:

> Ten years ago the larger private residences in New York were
> almost exclusively designed in a bastard combination of French
> and Italian and the refined qualities of both schools were lost in
> elaboration of overscaled ornament . . . The country as a whole
> is once more settling down into more sober realms of art . . . we
> are losing the attitude of mind which regarded the early Colonial
> architecture of this country as something to be admired but not
> imitated . . . The great firm of McKim, Mead & White never
> hesitated to borrow where they pleased and have executed with
> equal facility and success works in the most diverse styles, but . . .
> have mingled with the great volume of work executed occasional
> tonic doses of Colonial.[1]

PERCY PYNE HOUSE, PARK AVENUE BETWEEN EAST 68TH AND 69TH STREETS,
NEW YORK CITY, 1911.
PHOTOGRAPH BY JONATHAN WALLEN, 1997.

opposite

HARRY B. HOLLINS HOUSE, WEST 56TH STREET BETWEEN FIFTH AND SIXTH AVENUES,
NEW YORK CITY, 1901.

CHARLES DANA GIBSON HOUSE, EAST 73RD STREET BETWEEN PARK AND LEXINGTON
AVENUES, NEW YORK CITY, 1903.
PHOTOGRAPH BY JONATHAN WALLEN, 2007.

opposite

JAMES J. GOODWIN HOUSE, WEST 54TH STREET BETWEEN FIFTH AND SIXTH AVENUES,
NEW YORK CITY, 1898.

MOTT B. SCHMIDT

Mott B. Schmidt grew up in a brownstone neighborhood of Brooklyn. By the age of nine, he decided to become an architect, later augmenting his architectural education at Pratt Institute of Technology with a two-year Grand Tour of Europe. Returning to New York, he spent four years working in an architectural office before establishing his own practice. In 1920, after several years of working primarily on house renovations, Schmidt began to collaborate with the celebrated interior decorator Elsie de Wolfe on a series of projects that would establish him as both a significant architect and a practitioner sought after by members of New York's social elite. Schmidt's design of three townhouses on Sutton Place (formerly Avenue A) for Elizabeth Marbury, Anne Morgan, and Mrs. William K. Vanderbilt helped to make the area a stylish enclave. In contrast to the Georgian Revival work of established firms, principally McKim, Mead & White and Delano & Aldrich, Schmidt's work was visually simpler and employed a more exact use of American and English sources. The exterior design of Morgan's house at 3 Sutton Place was drawn from the eighteenth-century Samuel Powel and Benjamin Wistar Morris houses in Philadelphia.

　　Though Schmidt enjoyed professional success designing townhouses and country houses for socially prominent clients, as well as apartment buildings and civic buildings, his allegiance to traditional American and British precedents positioned him outside the mainstream of a profession that was increasingly pursuing Modernism. Completed in 1966, toward the end of his career, Schmidt's addition to Gracie Mansion—the late-eighteenth-century farmhouse that served as New York City's official mayoral residence—reflected his reputation as an accomplished historicist architect. The project also brought his work to the attention of a broader public. Schmidt died in 1977, just as a younger generation of architects was gaining an appreciation of a wide spectrum of traditional architectural vocabularies, particularly as articulated by American architects during the nineteenth and early twentieth centuries.

EMILY TREVOR HOUSE, EAST 90TH STREET BETWEEN FIFTH AND MADISON AVENUES, NEW YORK CITY, 1926.
PHOTOGRAPH BY PETER MAUSS/ESTO, 1987.

VIEW OF SUTTON PLACE BETWEEN EAST 57TH AND 58TH STREETS, NEW YORK CITY, SHOWING
MRS. WILLIAM K. VANDERBILT HOUSE, 1921, WITH ENTRANCE ON EAST 57TH STREET, AT FAR
RIGHT, WITH ANNE MORGAN HOUSE, 1921, SECOND FROM RIGHT, AND ELIZABETH MARBURY
HOUSE, 1920, SIXTH FROM RIGHT.
PHOTOGRAPH BY BERENICE ABBOTT, 1936.

DOORWAY OF ANNE MORGAN HOUSE
PHOTOGRAPH BY MARK ALAN HEWITT, C. 1985.

GARDENS OF MRS. WILLIAM K. VANDERBILT HOUSE (LEFT)
AND ANNE MORGAN HOUSE (RIGHT), SUTTON PLACE BETWEEN EAST 57TH AND
EAST 58TH STREETS, NEW YORK CITY, 1921.

One Sutton Place South, Cross & Cross and Rosario Candela, 1927, is visible in
background.

JOHN J. MCCLOY HOUSE, STAMFORD, CONNECTICUT, 1956.

POOK'S HILL (MOTT B. SCHMIDT HOUSE), BEDFORD, NEW YORK, 1926.
PHOTOGRAPH BY SAMUEL H. GOTTSCHO.

POOK'S HILL.

DWIGHT JAMES BAUM

Dwight James Baum designed buildings throughout the eastern United States—including the lavish Venetian-inspired mansion Cà d'Zan in Sarasota, Florida, for impresario John Ringling of the Ringling Bros. and Barnum & Bailey Circus—but he was best known in New York for 140 houses located in the Riverdale section of the Bronx where he lived and worked. Baum was born near Utica, New York, and studied architecture at Syracuse University; he subsequently worked for a number of New York–based architects, including McKim, Mead & White, before establishing his own practice.

Baum moved to Riverdale around 1912, building himself a Dutch Colonial house that contained an architectural office in the attic. Four years later, Baum renovated Fieldston Hill, home of the developer Edward Delafield. Baum subsequently became Delafield's architect of choice; Baum designed the Riverdale Country Club in a Dutch Colonial style, as well as many houses in a variety of idioms. Baum's extensive work in Riverdale, and particularly in the privately operated enclave of Fieldston, garnered widespread attention and helped to popularize the Colonial Revival as a cornerstone of the emerging suburban ideal. In 1931 Baum received a Gold Medal from Better Homes in America, an initiative begun by the Butterick Publishing Company in 1922 in the wake of the nation's housing shortage and later promoted by the federal government's National Better Homes Advisory Council. The medal was presented by President Herbert Hoover. In addition to his residential work, Baum codesigned the imposing Flushing Post Office in Queens, demonstrating that in his hands, the Colonial Revival style could be evocative of both cozy domesticity and civic authority.

SIMONE LA SALA HOUSE, FIELDSTON, BRONX, NEW YORK, 1930.
PHOTOGRAPH BY SAMUEL H. GOTTSCHO.

FIELDSTON, BRONX, NEW YORK, 1937.
PHOTOGRAPH BY SAMUEL H. GOTTSCHO.

HIRAM HALLE

Industrialist and businessman Hiram Halle created one of America's
most distinctive enclaves of Colonial Revival buildings in Pound Ridge,
New York, about an hour's drive from New York City. Combining
social activism and a passion for historic architecture, Halle bought
and renovated some forty old houses and additional buildings in Pound
Ridge and adjacent towns from 1928 through the late 1930s. To achieve
his wholesale transformation of simple buildings into livable, high-style
Colonial Revival structures, Halle opened a carpentry shop on his own
property, employing in the depths of the Depression about sixty locals to
rebuild the old structures, repair the area's old stone walls, and perform
other tasks in town. Halle's renovations were directed by master craftsman
Hermann Scheid, and architect Walter D. Gillooly provided design and
drafting services. Between 1936 and 1939, Halle also brought Jewish
exiles to work in Pound Ridge. Dedicated to Jewish causes, Halle had
also supported the University in Exile, an extension of the New School
for Social Research that brought intellectuals to America who had been
dismissed from their positions by the Nazi regime. While not following
modern standards of historic preservation, Halle nonetheless revitalized
the struggling farming community of Pound Ridge and turned it into
the wealthy suburb it is today.

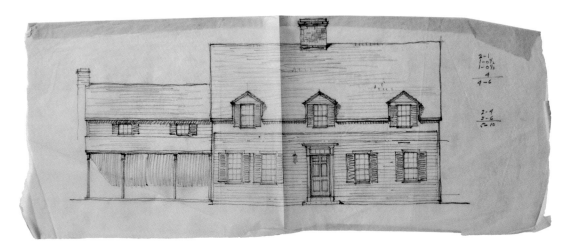

SKETCH OF HALLE-SALEM HOUSE RECONSTRUCTION (ABOVE AND OPPOSITE, BOTTOM LEFT),
POUND RIDGE, NEW YORK, 1930S.

Halle fabricated this house out of three existing structures: a 1756 farmhouse from North Salem,
New York, as well as a house from nearby Bedford and a barn from Danbury, Connecticut.
He updated this amalgam with historicist Colonial Revival details.

SKETCH OF HALLE-DEXTER LODGE, ALSO KNOWN AS EMILY SHAW'S INN (OPPOSITE ABOVE
AND BOTTOM RIGHT), POUND RIDGE, NEW YORK, 1930S.

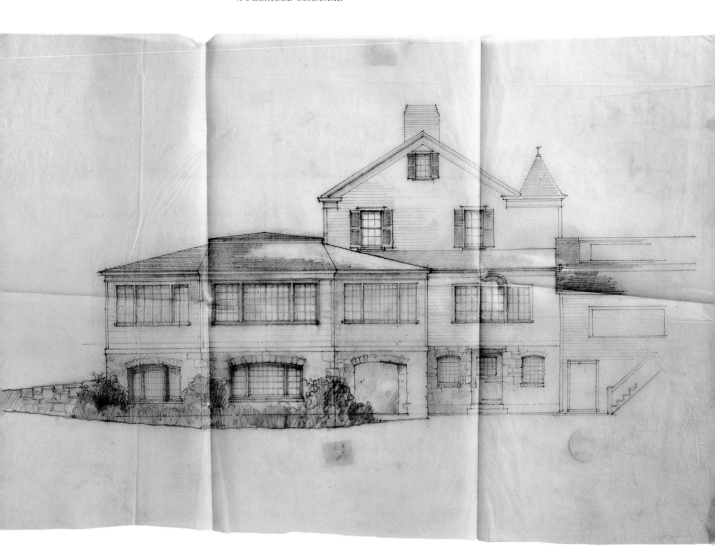

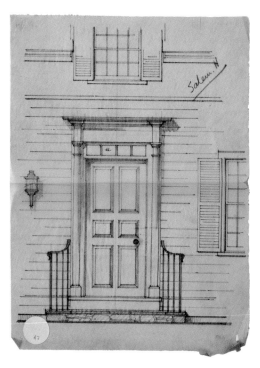

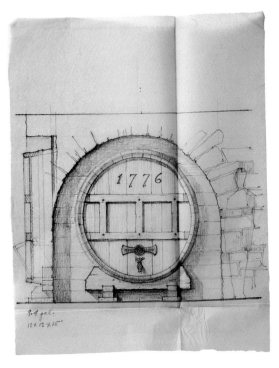

ROYAL BARRY WILLS

During the post–World War II era, Royal Barry Wills was arguably
the nation's most popular architect specializing in single-family houses.
Born outside of Boston and educated at the Massachusetts Institute
of Technology, Wills was initially employed in New York by the Turner
Construction Company as a design engineer and worked as an architect
in his spare hours. In 1925 Wills opened his own architectural office in
Boston, designing in a variety of historicist vocabularies, although in the
mid-1930s a member of the firm, the architect Hugh Stubbins, executed
a number of house commissions in the International Style. By this time,
Wills had specialized in the design of houses for a middle-class clientele.

In the postwar era, with the resurgence of the homebuilding
industry, Wills was perfectly positioned to become a leader in the field. By
1946 he had become the author of best-selling books on Colonial Revival
house design. The editors of *Life* succinctly stated that Wills designed "the
kind of house most Americans want."[2] Wills's work, which could be seen
throughout the New York region, had evolved from simpler schemes for
small houses to larger-scale full-blown essays in the Colonial Revival style,
complete with cobblestone-paved driveways. Wills used materials and
features closely associated with Colonial houses, including clapboard and
multipaned, double-hung, wood-framed windows. Wills also freely
interpreted such features as the covered wing connecting a typical New
England farmhouse to a barn, rendering it a kitchen and laundry room
linking the core of the house to a two-car garage. For the interiors of
his houses, which often incorporated dominant fireplaces, beamed
ceilings, wainscoting, and other traditional features, Wills would provide
his clients with decorating advice, including the purchase of Colonial
furniture or reproduction pieces. Though often dismissed by members of
the architectural profession, Wills was widely published in the popular
press and enjoyed enormous success; by the time of his death in 1962,
his firm had completed more than 2,500 house projects. The firm
continues today under his son, Richard Wills.

ROYAL BARRY WILLS PLANS FOR A SLOPE AND A VIEW

The Blackbourns *(see p. 50)* plan to build on a sloping lot which they now own, next to their present home. The shape and location of that lot, says Architect Wills, "practically dictates the plan of the house which they hope to build." The lot slopes down from the street toward Diamond Lake and a park which is being developed by the city. Hence Mr. Wills has a one-story front to face the street *(above)*, giving a cottage effect, and a three-story rear *(right)*. Living room, dining room and kitchen are placed in the rear, so that from them the Blackbourns may have a clear view of lake and park. Big casement windows also give the living and dining rooms plenty of sun and air.

Mr. Blackbourn's office is placed in the front of the house, adjoining the living room. The jog formed by the projection of the living room fireplace makes a space for his files. If and when Mr. Blackbourn moves to a downtown office, the office may become a study and the files be replaced by bookshelves.

Separated from the office by a handy first-floor lavatory is a guest room which could also be used as a maid's room or as an extra living room—welcome to Betty Jane and Bruce when they entertain their friends. On the second floor are three bedrooms, all with view of lake and park. In the bathroom, Mr. Wills has thoughtfully placed a cabinet for the Blackbourns' sun lamp. There are plenty of closets. One in the parents' bedroom could be turned into an extra bathroom later on.

The basement is divided between a laundry and heater and a recreation room with large windows and a door opening onto the grassy terrace in the rear.

The front of the house, Architect Wills directs, should be of whitewashed brick, with white-painted clapboards for sides and rear, green shutters, and roof of shingles weathered natural gray.

CONTINUED ON NEXT PAGE

"EIGHT HOUSES FOR MODERN LIVING," *LIFE* MAGAZINE, SEPTEMBER 26, 1938.

This issue of *Life* featured a twenty-three-page spread entitled "Eight Houses for Modern Living," designed for four representative American families earning two thousand to ten thousand dollars per year. Working with *Architectural Forum* magazine, *Life* selected eight architects to work on the project. A pair of architects designed for each family, one in a traditional style, one in a modern style. For the Blackbourn family of Minneapolis, Royal Barry Wills designed a traditional Colonial style home, while Frank Lloyd Wright designed one of his modern Usonian houses. The family chose Wills's design.

RUDOLPH JAY SCHAEFER HOUSE, MAMARONECK, NEW YORK, 1956.
PHOTOGRAPHS BY KEN DUPREY.

MODEL HOUSE FOR THE NEW YORK WORLD'S FAIR OF 1964, FLUSHING MEADOWS, QUEENS, NEW YORK.

JOSÉ MARIA ALLEGUE

José Maria Allegue was a custom homebuilder on Long Island's
South Shore. From the late 1940s through the 1960s, he produced
approximately thirty especially well-designed and finely crafted homes
primarily in the Colonial Revival style. John "Jack" Finn, although not
a licensed architect, designed many of the houses Allegue built. In her
book *José M. Allegue: A Builder's Legacy*, the architect and historian
Christine G. H. Franke has noted that "Finn was a highly trained designer
and capable architect, well versed in the popular Colonial Williamsburg
restoration architecture."[3]

CHARLES AND FRANCES GOLDBERGER HOUSE, HEWLETT BAY PARK, NEW YORK,
H. W. JOHANSEN AND MORTIMER FREEHOF / JOHN FINN, 1954.
PHOTOGRAPH BY KAREN A. DOMBROVSKI-SOBEL, 2001.

DINING ROOM WITH BUILT-IN CHINA CABINET, CHARLES AND FRANCES GOLDBERGER HOUSE.
PHOTOGRAPH BY KAREN A. DOMBROVSKI-SOBEL, 2001.

DEN WITH KNOTTY PINE WOOD PANELING, CHARLES AND FRANCES GOLDBERGER HOUSE.
PHOTOGRAPH BY KAREN DOMBROVSKI-SOBEL, 2001.

APARTMENT BUILDINGS

Colonial Revival apartment houses exerted strong "curb appeal" because of the widespread association with private houses. Even in a city where the percentage of residents living in multi-unit buildings was higher than anywhere else in the nation, and the majority of those residents rented rather than owned their apartments, the "house-proud" spirit of the nation still held sway. The design of large-scale Colonial-style apartment buildings, by leading residential architects including J.E.R. Carpenter, reflected the vocabulary's elasticity and its adaptability to urban conditions unimagined in the Colonial era. Colonial Revival ornamentation, as well as materials and colors associated with the style, were often brought inside apartment buildings and used in lobbies and common dining rooms, complete with appropriately articulated moldings and fireplaces, reproduction furniture, and themed wallpapers or murals.

JOHN MURRAY APARTMENTS, MADISON AVENUE AND EAST 37TH STREET, NEW YORK CITY, DEUTSEN & SHEA, C.1941. PHOTOGRAPH BY WURTS BROTHERS COMPANY.

DINING ROOM IN THE JOHN MURRAY APARTMENTS. PHOTOGRAPH BY WURTS BROTHERS COMPANY.

APARTMENT INTERIOR AT 18 GRAMERCY PARK, NEW YORK CITY, 1929.
PHOTOGRAPH BY SAMUEL H. GOTTSCHO.

The composition of this tableau, with its emphasis on the hearth, evokes Colonial Revival
photographs created by Wallace Nutting.

LOBBY AT 340 EAST 72ND STREET, BETWEEN FIRST AND SECOND AVENUES,
NEW YORK CITY, 1935.
PHOTOGRAPH BY SAMUEL H. GOTTSCHO.

CIVIC BUILDINGS

The grandly wrought Classicism that dominated the design of civic buildings in New York City during the so-called "American Renaissance" of the late nineteenth and early twentieth centuries, with its references to ancient Greece and Rome, often gave way during the interwar period to the Colonial Revival, with a different set of associations. The Colonial Revival could be read both as a reassertion of the country's core characteristics and values, used to instruct a newly diverse nation in the ways of citizenship, and an allusion to grassroots political organization, nostalgically suggesting a time when communities were smaller and democratic government more simply organized. The style was used by civic and political organizations, such as the League for Political Education and Tammany Hall, as well as by museums and by federal and municipal government in the form of borough halls and post offices. As applied to civic buildings, the Colonial Revival style was often immediately identifiable by slate-clad pitched roofs surmounted by cupolas.

MOUNT KISCO TOWN HALL, MOUNT KISCO, NEW YORK, MOTT B. SCHMIDT, 1932.
PHOTOGRAPH BY MARK ALAN HEWITT, C.1985.

MOUNT KISCO POST OFFICE, MOUNT KISCO, NEW YORK, MOTT B. SCHMIDT, 1936.
PHOTOGRAPH BY CERVIN ROBINSON, 1990.

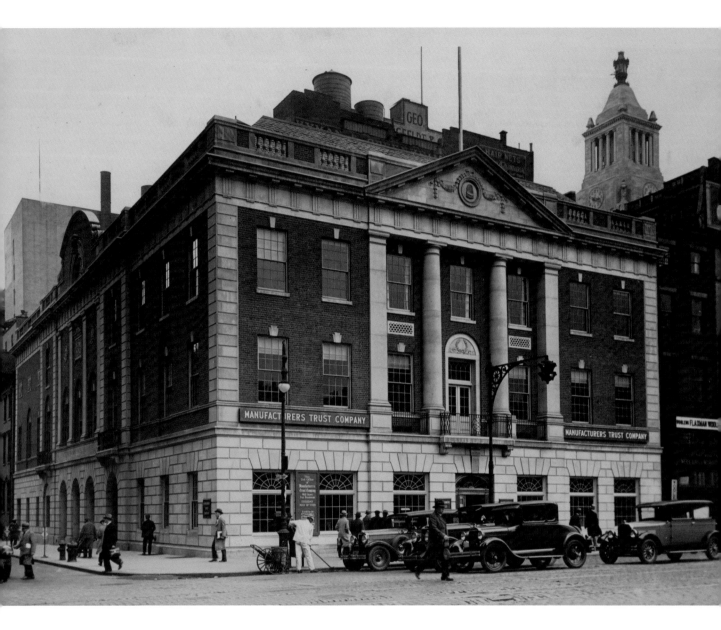

TAMMANY HALL, PARK AVENUE SOUTH AND EAST 17TH STREET, NEW YORK CITY,
THOMPSON, HOLMES & CONVERSE IN ASSOCIATION WITH CHARLES B. MEYERS, 1928.
PHOTOGRAPH BY EWING GALLOWAY.

While Tammany Hall's west facade fronting Union Square Park evoked Sir William Chambers's
Somerset House in London, it also resembled a building more directly related to
the political organization's history and mission: the original Federal Hall where George
Washington was inaugurated.

SKETCH OF PROPOSED TOWN HALL ADDITION BY LOUIS E. JALLADE,
PUBLISHED IN THE *NEW YORK TIMES*, APRIL 1, 1940.

In 1921 the League for Political Education completed the Georgian-style Town Hall, designed by Teunis J. van der Bent of McKim, Mead & White and located on West 43rd Street between Sixth Avenue and Broadway. In the late 1930s, a proposal by the architect Louis E. Jallade would have added five stories to the building and, on its roof, an open-air auditorium and a structure inspired by New England town halls to house administrative offices. A series of national forums to be held there would help Americans "make their privilege of free speech effective through a nationwide revival of the spirit of the old New England town meeting," according to Town Hall's president George V. Denny Jr. Jallade's design was never realized.[4]

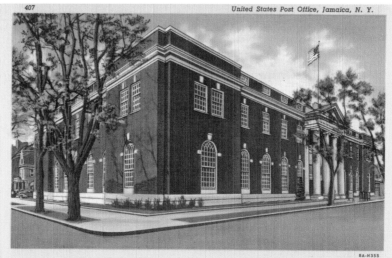

FLUSHING POST OFFICE, FLUSHING, QUEENS, NEW YORK, DWIGHT JAMES BAUM, 1932.
PHOTOGRAPH BY SAMUEL H. GOTTSCHO.

POSTCARD OF JAMAICA POST OFFICE, JAMAICA, QUEENS, NEW YORK, CROSS & CROSS, 1934.

opposite

LOBBY, GLEN COVE POST OFFICE, GLEN COVE, NEW YORK, DELANO & ALDRICH, 1933.
PHOTOGRAPH BY WURTS BROTHERS COMPANY.

ISLIP TOWN HALL, ISLIP, NEW YORK, EUGENE S. HELBIG, 1933.
PHOTOGRAPHS BY F. S. LINCOLN.

MUSEUM OF THE CITY OF NEW YORK

The idea of a museum devoted to New York was stimulated by Paris's Musée Carnavalet and spearheaded by Henry Collins Brown, author of numerous books on New York. Officially established in 1923, the museum was initially housed in the late-eighteenth-century Gracie Mansion, which the city provided. Plans for a new building of its own, however, were soon launched with a request for subscriptions. "The Museum of the City of New York," a subscription request noted, "has been established in response to an almost universal longing among our people, for some place in which to preserve the annals and records of their own home town."[5] Among the museum's earliest efforts was the *Old New York* exhibition held at the Fine Arts Building in 1926.

On Monday, January 11, 1932—coincident with the birthday of Alexander Hamilton—4,386 people celebrated the opening of the museum's new home on Fifth Avenue. The museum's five-story, red-brick Colonial Revival building, designed by Joseph H. Freedlander, featured a portico replicating Federal Hall. (Freedlander had won a limited competition, vying against such New York architects as Delano & Aldrich and Grosvenor Atterbury, among others.) The exterior's Colonial Revival theme continued inside, where visitors explored the city's history through a variety of visual means. Sixteen dioramas created by Dwight Franklin and Ned J. Burns replicated in miniature such early New York scenes as the purchase of Manhattan Island and Washington's inauguration, while a large model by Charles Capehart depicted New Amsterdam in 1660. Other displays included costumes and New York silver arranged by curator V. Isabelle Miller, who had joined the museum's staff from the Metropolitan Museum of Art. In 1937 Miller organized *Silver by New York Makers, Late 17th Century to 1900*, a pioneering exhibition that chronologically presented the development of American silver; the exhibition furthered connoisseurship and added to the growing recognition of the aesthetic significance of early American decorative arts.

MUSEUM OF THE CITY OF NEW YORK, FIFTH AVENUE BETWEEN EAST 103RD AND 104TH
STREETS, JOSEPH H. FREEDLANDER, 1932.
PHOTOGRAPH BY SAMUEL H. GOTTSCHO.

ENTRANCE HALL, MUSEUM OF THE CITY OF NEW YORK.
PHOTOGRAPH BY SAMUEL H. GOTTSCHO.

SECOND FLOOR GALLERIES, MUSEUM OF THE CITY OF NEW YORK.
PHOTOGRAPH BY SAMUEL H. GOTTSCHO.

DIORAMA OF FRAUNCES TAVERN, MUSEUM OF THE CITY OF NEW YORK, C. 1932.

NED J. BURNS MODELING BLUE BELL TAVERN DIORAMA,
MUSEUM OF THE CITY OF NEW YORK, C. 1932.

DIORAMA SHOWING GEORGE WASHINGTON'S INAUGURATION IN LOWER MANHATTAN
IN 1789, MUSEUM OF THE CITY OF NEW YORK, C. 1932.

COLONIAL REVIVAL DOLLHOUSE, MUSEUM OF THE CITY OF NEW YORK, 1930S.

This fully furnished dollhouse was made by Fordham W. Briggs, who constructed it while working on a set of dioramas for the museum.

Presentation of Plan

VILLAGE GREEN

and

SHOPPING CENTER

Stony Brook, Long Island

PRESENTATION OF PLAN: VILLAGE GREEN AND SHOPPING CENTER,
STONY BROOK, NEW YORK, JANUARY 14, 1940.

STONY BROOK VILLAGE

Envisioned in the late 1930s by shoe manufacturer Ward Melville, the village green and town center of Stony Brook on Long Island looked to both the community's own Colonial past and the restored Colonial town of Williamsburg, Virginia. Melville hired the architect Richard Haviland Smythe to restore existing buildings, remove stylistically inappropriate ones, and create new buildings in a Colonial Revival style. The development, completed in 1941, took the shape of a crescent and incorporated a post office, firehouse, courthouse, and shops. Deliveries and garbage collection were handled largely out of sight, behind the rows of connected commercial buildings. Stony Brook's pedestrian-friendly village atmosphere stood in marked contrast to the automobile-centric shopping centers and strip malls that would soon become a standard feature of suburbs nationwide.

POSTCARD OF STONY BROOK POST OFFICE, C.1941.

POSTCARD OF STONY BROOK VILLAGE SHOPPING CENTER, C.1941.

CLUBS AND ASSOCIATIONS

In the hands of leading architects such as McKim, Mead & White, Delano & Aldrich, and Cross & Cross, among others, the Colonial Revival style, having strong associations with both domesticity and civism, seemed to perfectly express the role of the private club in the city's social life, serving as both a refuge from home life and a bastion of exclusivity. The style was also employed by associations established to serve the needs of the poor.

ABRONS ARTS CENTER PLAYHOUSE, FORMERLY THE NEIGHBORHOOD PLAYHOUSE,
GRAND AND PITT STREETS, NEW YORK CITY,
HARRY C. INGALLS AND F. BURRALL HOFFMAN JR., 1915.

The Neighborhood Playhouse was created by the socially progressive
Henry Street Settlement.

ABRONS ARTS CENTER PLAYHOUSE, J. LAWRENCE JONES AND ASSOCIATES,
RESTORATION ARCHITECTS. 1996.
PHOTOGRAPH BY PAUL LA ROSA, 2010.

NATIONAL SOCIETY OF COLONIAL DAMES, EAST 71ST STREET BETWEEN SECOND AND
THIRD AVENUES, NEW YORK CITY, RICHARD HENRY DANA JR., 1930.
PHOTOGRAPH BY SAMUEL H. GOTTSCHO.

CHROMOLITHOGRAPH BY JENNIE BROWNSCOMBE OF WALL STREET DURING THE COLONIAL PERIOD, SHOWING BUILDINGS THAT SERVED AS AN INSPIRATION FOR THE NATIONAL SOCIETY OF COLONIAL DAMES HEADQUARTERS.

HARVARD CLUB.
PHOTOGRAPH BY EDUARD HUEBER, 1986.

HARVARD CLUB, WEST 44TH STREET BETWEEN FIFTH AND SIXTH AVENUES, NEW YORK CITY,
MCKIM, MEAD & WHITE, 1894; ADDITIONS 1905 AND 1915.
PHOTOGRAPH BY AMERICAN STUDIO, 1920.

COLONY CLUB, MADISON AVENUE BETWEEN EAST 30TH AND 31ST STREETS, NEW YORK CITY,
MCKIM, MEAD & WHITE, 1908.
PHOTOGRAPH BY WURTS BROTHERS COMPANY.

COLONY CLUB.
PHOTOGRAPHS BY JONATHAN WALLEN, 2007.

DELANO & ALDRICH

Delano & Aldrich, founded by William Adams Delano and Chester Holmes Aldrich, was one of the nation's most prominent and prolific architectural firms during the first half of the twentieth century. Both partners had been educated at the Ecole des Beaux-Arts in Paris and had been mentored by the architect Thomas Hastings as young practitioners in the firm of Carrère & Hastings. Delano & Aldrich excelled at interpreting and adopting models from Colonial America or the early Republic. In New York City, the architects dominated one building type more than any other: clubhouses. As early as the end of World War I, Delano & Aldrich had surpassed the era's most well-known firm, McKim, Mead & White, as the architects of choice for New York's most prestigious social clubs.

INTERIOR OF THE KNICKERBOCKER CLUB.
PHOTOGRAPH BY JONATHAN WALLEN, 2001.

KNICKERBOCKER CLUB, FIFTH AVENUE AND EAST 62ND STREET, NEW YORK CITY, 1913.
PHOTOGRAPH BY WURTS BROTHERS COMPANY.

As a young architect, William Adams Delano designed a facility for the Knickerbocker Club, an offshoot of the Union Club, in the Federalist style. Delano wrote, "I felt the elaborate facades of the prevalent French School did not fit in New York," and he drew inspiration instead from the more understated expression of his father's Greek Revival townhouse at 12 Washington Square. Delano would later state that the house had a great influence on my architectural thinking.[6]

GREENWICH HOUSE, BARROW STREET BETWEEN WEST FOURTH STREET AND
SEVENTH AVENUE, NEW YORK CITY, 1917.

In contrast to the exclusive social clubs for which Delano & Aldrich were famous, the firm
designed facilities for social service organizations.

KIPS BAY BOYS CLUB, EAST 52ND STREET BETWEEN FIRST AND SECOND AVENUES,
NEW YORK CITY, 1931.
PHOTOGRAPH BY WURTS BROTHERS COMPANY.

SCHOOLS AND CAMPUSES

The didactic dimension of the Colonial Revival, in which the style was employed to instruct building users and passersby in aspects of the American experience and national character, was perhaps nowhere more appropriate than in the design of schools. In the interwar period, some public school architects rejected the Dutch Gothic style, previously advanced by New York City School Superintendent and architect C. B. J. Snyder, in favor of Colonial Revival. Private schools and universities also employed refined and understated interpretations of the style.

ABIGAIL ADAMS SCHOOL, 84TH AVENUE BETWEEN 170TH AND 172ND STREETS, JAMAICA HILLS, QUEENS, NEW YORK, 1939.

GEORGE WASHINGTON HIGH SCHOOL, AUDUBON AVENUE AND WEST 190TH STREET,
NEW YORK CITY, WILLIAM H. GOMPERT, 1925.
PHOTOGRAPH BY WURTS BROTHERS COMPANY.

JAMAICA HIGH SCHOOL, GOTHIC DRIVE AND 168TH STREET, JAMAICA, QUEENS, NEW YORK,
WILLIAM H. GOMPERT, 1927.

BENJAMIN FRANKLIN HIGH SCHOOL, EAST RIVER DRIVE BETWEEN EAST 114TH AND
116TH STREETS, NEW YORK CITY, ERIC KEBBON, 1941.
PHOTOGRAPH BY WURTS BROTHERS COMPANY.

JEWISH THEOLOGICAL SEMINARY, BROADWAY AND WEST 122ND STREET, NEW YORK CITY,
WILLIAM GEHRON, 1930.
PHOTOGRAPH BY PEYSER AND PATZIG.

VANDERBILT LAW SCHOOL, NEW YORK UNIVERSITY, NEW YORK CITY, WASHINGTON SQUARE
SOUTH BETWEEN SULLIVAN AND MACDOUGAL STREETS, EGGERS & HIGGINS, 1951.
PHOTOGRAPH BY WILLIAM R. SIMMONS.

CHURCHES AND RELIGIOUS BUILDINGS

The design of urban churches, so strongly associated with Gothic architecture throughout the nineteenth century, increasingly incorporated the Colonial Revival during the interwar period. Synagogues also adopted the style, perhaps as a reflection of increased assimilation, particularly in suburban settings.

LARCHMONT TEMPLE, LARCHMONT, NEW YORK, SCHUMAN & LICHTENSTEIN ARCHITECTS,
1954/PASANELLA, KLEIN, STOLZMAN, BERG ARCHITECTS, 2002.
PHOTOGRAPH BY ZE'EV AVIEZER, 2010.

When the members of the Reform Jewish congregation of the Larchmont Temple decided to build a new synagogue, they chose a Colonial Revival design that would, they stated, "integrate architecturally with the surrounding community."[7]

BRICK PRESBYTERIAN CHURCH, PARK AVENUE AND 91ST STREET, NEW YORK CITY,
YORK & SAWYER, 1938.

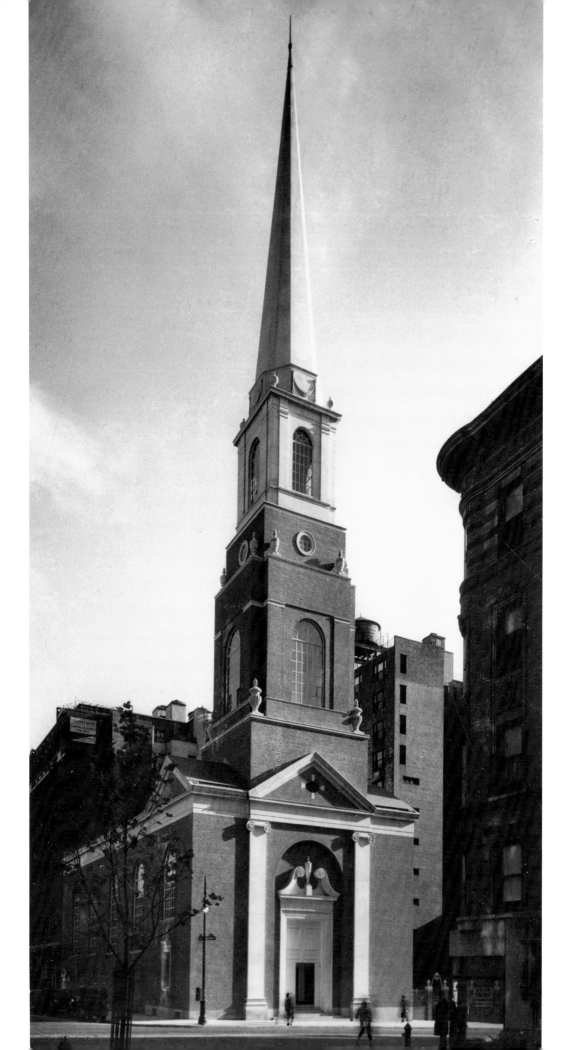

EIGHTH CHURCH OF CHRIST, SCIENTIST, EAST 77TH STREET BETWEEN PARK AND
LEXINGTON AVENUES, NEW YORK CITY, C. DALE BADGELEY, 1951.
PHOTOGRAPH BY GOTTSCHO-SCHLEISNER, INC.

C. Dale Badgeley's design for the Eighth Church of Christ, Scientist synthesized elements of
a Colonial Revival vocabulary, including red brick, with a Modernist sensibility of streamlined,
unornamented surfaces.

opposite

UNITARIAN CHURCH OF ALL SOULS, LEXINGTON AVENUE AND EAST 80TH STREET,
NEW YORK CITY, HOBART UPJOHN, 1932.

COMMERCIAL BUILDINGS

The Colonial Revival was used for a wide variety of commercial buildings. For banks, the style evoked associations with the nation's past to reassure investors that their assets were in good hands. For midpriced restaurant chains, the Colonial Revival evoked feelings of a cozy domesticity defined by home-style cooking and unpretentious service, sometimes carrying the motif as far as the waitresses' uniforms.

BANK OF MANHATTAN BRANCH, MADISON AVENUE AND EAST 64TH STREET, NEW YORK CITY, MORRELL SMITH, 1932.

SKETCH OF THE QUEENSBORO CORPORATION OFFICES, 37TH AVENUE AND 79TH STREET, JACKSON HEIGHTS, QUEENS, NEW YORK, ANDREW J. THOMAS, 1948.

MIXED-USE COMMERCIAL AND RESIDENTIAL BUILDING, MADISON AVENUE BETWEEN
EAST 64TH AND 65TH STREETS, NEW YORK CITY, ROUSE & GOLDSTONE, 1918.

This Federal-style-inspired building occupied the former site of the B'Nai Jeshrun Synagogue
(Rafael Guastavino and Schwarzmann & Buchman, 1885) and internally retained features
of the synagogue.

POSTCARD OF THE COLONIAL ROOM AT THE ROOSEVELT HOTEL,
MADISON AVENUE AT 45TH STREET, NEW YORK CITY,
GEORGE B. POST AND LYMAN W. CLEVELAND, 1924.

POSTCARD OF KEW GARDENS INN, KEW GARDENS, QUEENS, NEW YORK. NO DATE.

COLONIAL HOUSE, 158-06 NORTHERN BOULEVARD, FLUSHING, L. I.   E-4030

HOWARD JOHNSON'S RESTAURANT, NORTHERN BOULEVARD, QUEENS, NEW YORK, 1939.
PHOTOGRAPH BY WURTS BROTHERS COMPANY.

opposite

HOWARD JOHNSON'S RESTAURANT, QUEENS BOULEVARD, QUEENS, NEW YORK.
JOSEPH G. MORGAN, WITH NEW YORK WORLD'S FAIR OF 1939/40 BEYOND.

POSTCARD, COLONIAL HOUSE RESTAURANT, FLUSHING, NEW YORK, NO DATE.

STOUFFER'S RESTAURANT — 540 Fifth Avenue, New York City

STOUFFER'S RESTAURANT, FIFTH AVENUE BETWEEN WEST 44TH AND 45TH STREETS,
NEW YORK CITY, DWIGHT JAMES BAUM, C.1937.
PHOTOGRAPH BY SAMUEL H. GOTTSCHO.

POSTCARD OF STOUFFER'S RESTAURANT.

INTERIOR OF STOUFFER'S RESTAURANT.
PHOTOGRAPH BY SAMUEL H. GOTTSCHO.

FRAUNCES TAVERN

Etienne DeLancey built a house on the current site of Fraunces Tavern
in 1719. In 1762 the house was purchased by Samuel Fraunces, who
converted it into a tavern. After British troops left New York City in
defeat, General George Washington addressed the victorious officers
of the Continental Army at a farewell dinner at the tavern. In 1907,
following several fires and reconstructions of the existing structure,
architect William Mersereau completed an extensive renovation in a
Colonial Revival style. While Mersereau claimed to follow the roofline
of the original building, without extant images of the original,
the accuracy of the new design is questionable.

POSTCARD OF FRAUNCES TAVERN SHOWING 1907 RESTORATION OF ORIGINAL DINING ROOM.

POSTCARD OF FRAUNCES TAVERN, PEARL AND BROAD STREETS, NEW YORK CITY,
BEFORE RESTORATION IN 1907.

POSTCARD OF FRAUNCES TAVERN, AFTER RESTORATION.

COLONIAL
CHIC

DECORATIVE ARTS

SYPHER & CO.

Sypher & Co. was a New York City purveyor of furniture and other decorative arts established as early as 1840. When the craze for old-time reproductions erupted after the 1876 Centennial, Sypher & Co. built a four-story structure where it employed about fifty people to meet consumer demand for the new style. To help his customers grasp how such furniture could be used in their houses, the firm's head, Obadiah Sypher, created pioneering examples of demonstration room settings in the basement of his new facility at 860 Broadway, starting in 1884.

ARMCHAIR MADE BY SYPHER & CO., MAHOGANY AND MODERN
LEATHER UPHOLSTERY, 1880–83.

The form and details of this mahogany armchair looked back to Chippendale-inspired furniture created in Philadelphia in the eighteenth century.

CORNER CUPBOARD MADE BY SYPHER & CO.,
MAHOGANY AND PINE, 1875–90.

R. J. HORNER & COMPANY

The retail store and factory of Robert J. Horner was located on West 23rd Street off Fifth Avenue when the company created this desk. Inspired by an eighteenth-century Chippendale slant-top desk, the late-nineteenth-century Horner version added a floral mother-of-pearl inlay on the desk's top. In decorating their homes, customers could consult Horner's booklet *How to Furnish Our American Homes.*

ADVERTISEMENT FOR R. J. HORNER & COMPANY, 1887.

DESK MADE BY R. J. HORNER & COMPANY,
WOOD AND MOTHER-OF-PEARL INLAY, 1890–95.

ERNEST F. HAGEN

Ernest F. Hagen played an important role in the Colonial Revival, not only by documenting, but also by restoring and reinterpreting in his own furniture that of Duncan Phyfe, one of early America's preeminent cabinetmakers. Hagen moved from Germany to New York City with his family in 1844, and in 1858 he formed a partnership with Matthew Meier under the name of Meier and Hagen. Although the firm produced furniture in many styles, Hagen took special interest in the work of Phyfe, even acquiring his tools and templates. "It's almost as if Duncan Phyfe put his tools down one day," curator Christopher Monkhouse told the *New York Times* in 1996, "and Ernest Hagen picked them up the next."[1]

Hagen also advanced the American taste for Duncan Phyfe through means other than his furniture. His writings such as "Duncan Phyfe Notes" recorded his research and laid the groundwork for twentieth-century scholarship on Phyfe. In 1909 Hagen worked with R. T. Haines Halsey, later a key figure in the creation of the Metropolitan Museum of Art's American Wing, to assemble furniture attributed to Phyfe's workshop for the museum's *Hudson-Fulton Exhibition of American Industrial Arts* that year. After Hagen's death, his studio played a part in the 1922 exhibition entitled *Furniture Masterpieces of Duncan Phyfe*, which was noteworthy as the first museum presentation focused on a single American cabinetmaker.

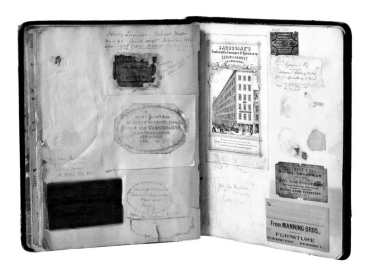

SCRAPBOOK COMPILED BY ERNEST F. HAGEN, 1892–1906.

FURNITURE MASTERPIECES OF DUNCAN PHYFE EXHIBITION,
METROPOLITAN MUSEUM OF ART, 1922.

SOFA MADE BY DUNCAN PHYFE BETWEEN 1810 AND 1815, AND RESTORED IN THE SHOP OF
ERNEST F. HAGEN, 1922, MAHOGANY, TULIP POPLAR, PINE, WITH MODERN UPHOLSTERY (1964).

That this sofa was restored in 1922, probably by Hagen's son Frederick, suggests it was featured
in the Metropolitan Museum of Art's 1922 Phyfe exhibition.

SOFA MADE BY ERNEST F. HAGEN, MAHOGANY AND CANE, C. 1898.

MUSIC CHAIR LABELED BY ERNEST F. HAGEN, MAHOGANY WITH OAK, 1901.

SIDE CHAIR BY ERNEST F. HAGEN FURNITURE AND ANTIQUES; MAHOGANY, METAL,
AND MODERN DAMASK UPHOLSTERY; C.1926.

This chair carefully reproduces a famous Phyfe design with its elegant lyre-shaped back inset.

ELEANOR ROOSEVELT'S VAL-KILL

On May 16, 1927, Eleanor Roosevelt, soon to be First Lady of New York State and eventually the nation, opened her East Side townhouse to a public viewing of reproductions of eighteenth-century American furnishings made by the Val-Kill Industries. Founded in 1926 by Mrs. Roosevelt and three friends—Nancy Cook, Marion Dickerman, and Caroline O'Day—this enterprise was located near the Roosevelt family home in Hyde Park, New York. Its goal was to provide training and jobs to local men and women in handcrafted manufacturing ideally keeping them in rural Hyde Park rather than letting them go off to factory work in New York City. Until the operation closed in 1936, Val-Kill employees produced replicas of early American furniture, pewter, and weavings. Many of the pieces were reproductions from museums, and Val-Kill products were carried by leading department stores and specialty shops in various American cities.

ELEANOR ROOSEVELT SHOWING VAL-KILL FURNITURE IN NEW YORK CITY, 1933.

For this exhibition and sale of Val-Kill furniture, two floors of the Roosevelt house in New York were emptied and refurnished.

PEWTER CREAMER AND SUGAR BOWL MADE BY ARNOLD BERGE IN VAL-KILL FORGE, 1934–38.

PAIR OF PEWTER CANDLESTICKS MADE BY ARNOLD BERGE IN VAL-KILL FORGE, 1934–38.

MAPLE BUTTERFLY TABLE MADE BY FRANK LANDOLFA FOR VAL-KILL SHOP, C. 1928.

PINE CHEST OF DRAWERS MADE FOR VAL-KILL SHOP, 1927–36.

NANCY VINCENT McCLELLAND

Nancy Vincent McClelland advanced the appeal of American Colonial and Federal-era decoration through her efforts as a designer, author, and antiques expert. Initially working as a reporter for a Philadelphia newspaper and a display designer for the city's Wanamaker's department store, in 1913 McClelland opened Au Quatrième, a specialty decorating shop located within Wanamaker's New York City store. Focusing largely on European decorative arts, Au Quatrième also sold American Colonial antiques, including pieces amassed by Wallace Nutting.

In 1922 McClelland opened her own business, which specialized in French designs but continued to promulgate the taste for American Colonial. McClelland was especially known for her interest in wallpaper. She sold modern and historic wallpapers, reproductions were made in France specifically for her firm, and the first of her many books, *Historic Wall-papers: From Their Inception to the Introduction of Machinery* (1924) surveyed collections in the United States and Europe. In 1937 she supplied wallpapers for the new Williamsburg Inn at Colonial Williamsburg, and in 1939 she created modern scenic wallpaper inspired by Washington's inauguration. McClelland's other books included *Furnishing the Colonial and Federal House* (1936) and *Duncan Phyfe and the English Regency, 1795–1830* (1939).

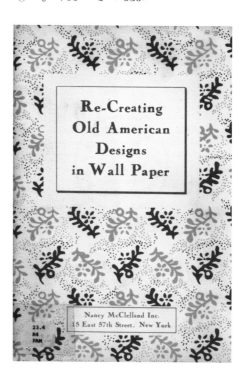

NANCY McCLELLAND, *RE-CREATING OLD AMERICAN DESIGNS IN WALL PAPER*,
NANCY McCLELLAND, INC., 1941.

GEORGE WASHINGTON IN MASONIC TRIANGLE WALLPAPER,
NANCY MCCLELLAND, INC., 1950S.

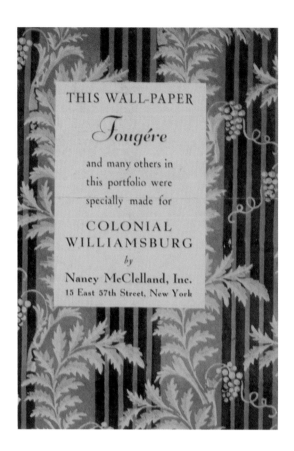

ADVERTISEMENT FOR NANCY MCCLELLAND, INC., *HOUSE AND GARDEN*, NOVEMBER 1937.

This advertisement illustrated a wallpaper made by McClelland for Colonial Williamsburg and exhibited at her Manhattan shop.

FOYER, BRICK HOUSE, SHELBURNE FARMS, VERMONT, 2010.

From 1913 to 1960, Brick House was the Vermont home of Electra Havemeyer Webb and her husband, James Watson Webb. In her early years of residence, Mrs. Webb added on to the house and converted it into her own personal museum of Colonial-era artifacts. As these collections grew, the idea of today's Shelburne Museum emerged: a complex of historic buildings housing early American artifacts and period rooms, some done in collaboration with collector and decorator Katherine Prentiss Murphy. The recent restoration of Brick House features Nancy McClelland's Feather wallpaper in the foyer.

JACOB MARGOLIS

As businessmen and woodworkers, brothers Jacob, Nathan, and Reuben Margolis played various important roles in promoting the Colonial Revival. Immigrating to the United States from today's Lithuania (Israel Sack's birthplace as well), they settled in Hartford, Connecticut. Nathan, who came to America in 1893, established a business with his father repairing furniture and eventually buying and selling antiques and making reproductions. Reuben also worked as a cabinetmaker in Hartford, and at the height of the antiques craze of the 1920s, he traveled extensively to London in search of material for the American market. In addition to selling to Israel Sack, Reuben also found furniture for his brother Jacob, who had become a dealer in Hartford and moved to New York City in 1898–99. In the 1920s, Jacob held publicized auctions of high-end antiques in Manhattan. Jacob provided repair services as well, and he offered advice to leading collectors, to whom his training as a cabinetmaker proved helpful in determining whether pieces were authentic or fake. Jacob also made reproductions of early American furniture, increasing this part of his business after 1927. In his use of old woods and hand-workmanship, Margolis identified himself as superior to such competitors as Wallace Nutting, W. & J. Sloane, and Erskine-Danforth.

EARLY AMERICAN FURNITURE

A Fine Collection of Choice Pieces Always on View

MARGOLIS SHOP

1132 *Madison Avenue*, NEW YORK CITY

THREE BLOCKS FROM THE AMERICAN WING OF THE METROPOLITAN MUSEUM

ADVERTISEMENT FOR JACOB MARGOLIS, *THE MAGAZINE ANTIQUES*, NOVEMBER 1924.

MAPLE-FRAMED MIRROR MADE BY JACOB MARGOLIS, 1929.

MAHOGANY DINING TABLE MADE BY JACOB MARGOLIS, 1929.

This dining table was one of ninety pieces commissioned by collector Francis P. Garvan
for the Yale Art Gallery.

DANERSK FURNITURE

The Erskine-Danforth Corporation of New York was in business from 1914 until the early years of the Depression. Its line of traditional, most notably Colonial Revival, furniture marketed under the name "Danersk," while not stylistically adventurous, was nonetheless very popular with both homeowners and business executives. Advertisements and promotional booklets with such titles as *How to Know Good Furniture as Interpreted by Danersk* stressed that the company offered "true distinction, charm and value." Many pieces were inspired by study of early American furniture at the Metropolitan Museum of Art and were advertised as "furniture that brings the joy of collecting and yet meets the demands of today."[2] Other marketing materials often stressed the designer pedigree of a reproduced piece: Duncan Phyfe tables and Samuel McIntire tables and a Hepplewhite armchair were included in a 1924 furniture price list. Danersk furniture was also available through showrooms in New York and other cities from Chicago to Los Angeles, which displayed demonstration rooms combining Danersk furniture, block prints, and chintzes.

ART-IN-TRADES CLUB YEARBOOK, NEW YORK, 1923.

This yearbook was published in conjunction with the Art-in-Trades Club's annual exhibition. In 1923 the exhibition presented tableaux of early American furniture and reproductions manufactured by Erskine-Danforth.

DANERSK ADVERTISEMENT, *THE MAGAZINE ANTIQUES*, JANUARY 1932.

NOT TO SUPPLANT HEIRLOOMS OF THE PAST, BUT TO MAINTAIN THE INTEGRITY OF A RICH TRADITION

A *chair*

THAT BECAME A *bed*

ALL through Colonial New England, and up and down the Hudson, early American craftsmen showed a preference for the friendly ladder-back chair. From Holland came the original chairs of this simple and charming type.

But it was a Danersk craftsman who conceived the first ladder-back bed. He placed two handsome ladder-back chairs together, and lo, a new creation was born. Thus do our master craftsmen enrich the fine traditions of the past, not by slavish copying of the pieces of an earlier day but by re-creating with understanding and respect for the past, and with equal consideration for the conditions of modern living.

Every Danersk piece is designed and fashioned to fulfil its function perfectly in a *modern* home. All of the changing factors of modern heating and modern social custom are taken into careful account in every piece of furniture that we build. That's why Danersk finishes do not crack and peel, Danersk woods do not warp, and Danersk drawers do not stick.

Structurally, any Danersk "heirloom of tomorrow" would we believe gladden the hearts of Samuel MacIntire, of Salem, of Thomas Chippendale and of all those great cabinetmakers of the past who built as we build, with scrupulous honesty, with painstaking care, and the skill and understanding of masters.

Our 300 Scotch and English craftsmen work with tools and facilities superior in fact to those of the past, and with the increased knowledge that modern science has brought. For these reasons they build choice furniture more economically than pieces of equal value have ever before been built, and do it without resort to any of the shortcuts of mass-built furniture.

The gracious comfort of Danersk pieces — the sheer joy that they add to living — are real and enduring things which long outlive their owners. For Danersk Furniture grows mellower — actually more desirable — with age.

You will find a visit to our showrooms a delightful and worthwhile experience. Upon request we will be glad to send you a copy of our 72-page illustrated booklet, "How to Know Good Furniture." It is filled with many valuable hints on the care and preservation of antique as well as modern furniture.

DANERSK FURNITURE

ERSKINE-DANFORTH CORPORATION   *Designers and makers of choice furniture*

NEW YORK: 383 MADISON AVENUE

CHICAGO: 620 NORTH MICHIGAN AVENUE   LOS ANGELES: 2869 WEST 7TH STREET

ONEIDACRAFT AND COMPANY OF MASTER CRAFTSMEN

Department store W. & J. Sloane was especially active not only in retailing Colonial Revival furniture, but also in its manufacture. To produce their own examples, Sloane founded two companies in the 1920s: the Company of Master Craftsmen, with a factory in Flushing, Queens, and the Oneidacraft Company in Oneida, New York. The curator of the Metropolitan Museum of Art's American Wing, R. T. Haines Halsey, was president of Oneidacraft in the mid-1920s. In addition to promoting their furniture through advertisements, W. & J. Sloane sometimes featured pieces in its House of Years, a series of full-scale demonstration rooms.

RENDERING OF COMPANY OF MASTER CRAFTSMEN FACTORY, FLUSHING, QUEENS, NEW YORK, 1925.

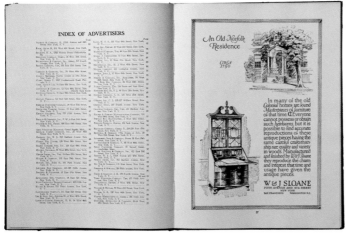

ADVERTISEMENT FOR W. & J. SLOANE/COMPANY OF MASTER CRAFTSMEN,
THE MAGAZINE ANTIQUES, JUNE 1927.

ADVERTISEMENT FOR W. & J. SLOANE, ART-IN-TRADES CLUB YEARBOOK, 1923.

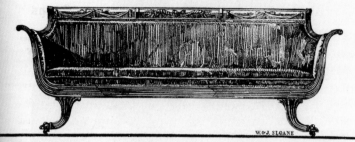

DUNCAN PHYFE FURNITURE

THE term *Duncan Phyfe* is not—like the terms Chippendale, Sheraton, and so on, — properly applicable to a general furniture style, but only to the specific examples of furniture which were made in Phyfe's own shop under the master's personal direction, or to the replicas of them. For Duncan Phyfe was really one of many interpreters of the style popularized by Thomas Sheraton. His merit lies less in the originality of his designs than in the supreme skill with which he utilized motives already accepted.

Born in Scotland in 1768, Phyfe came to America as a lad, and, in New York City, built up an important trade as cabinetmaker to the first families of the growing financial metropolis. His furniture is characterized by an extraordinary perfection of workmanship, great refinement of general proportions and rare exquisiteness of detail, coupled with an almost unapproachable particularity in the selection and matching of woods.

In reproducing Duncan Phyfe models, therefore, the modern maker may be permitted no liberties in design, no short cuts in manufacture, since even slight deviations from the letter of the master's work entail the almost complete extinction of its spirit.

Had Duncan Phyfe, himself, supervised the making of the sofa here illustrated the finished work could hardly have been different. For that fact more than conscientious effort is responsible. In the products of this Company of Master Craftsmen, good intentions are substantiated by appreciation of the excellence of fine early models and by a profound knowledge of the means by which, in each instance, superior quality was achieved.

Sole Selling Agents

W. & J. SLOANE

575 FIFTH AVENUE

NEW YORK CITY

ADVERTISEMENT FOR W. & J. SLOANE/COMPANY OF MASTER CRAFTSMEN,
THE MAGAZINE ANTIQUES, SEPTEMBER 1926.

SETTEE MANUFACTURED BY THE COMPANY OF MASTER CRAFTSMEN,
MAHOGANY AND UPHOLSTERY, C. 1926.

NEW YORK STATE HISTORICAL ASSOCIATION'S RECREATION OF THE JOHN HANCOCK HOUSE,
TICONDEROGA, NEW YORK, 1926.

This house featured reproduction furniture provided by W. & J. Sloane.

WARREN MCARTHUR

Warren McArthur was a furniture designer and manufacturer whose business office was located in New York City from around 1933 until his death. McArthur's patented manufacturing process of standard aluminum tubular parts and mechanical joinery allowed him to produce over 1,600 different designs including this streamlined version of a Colonial-era ladder-back chair. Its rainbow hues resulted from a process patented in 1931 by DuPont, which impregnated the aluminum with mineral dyes that sealed the surface in colors such as bronze, red, yellow, orange, gold, or ebony. In marketing his chairs, tables, and other furnishings, McArthur assured potential customers that his work was up-to-date in its industrial materials and modular construction methods, yet traditional in its finish—"an aristocratic silver satin surface—non-glaring—that harmonizes with any decorative scheme."[3]

CHAIR DESIGNED BY WARREN MCARTHUR,
ANODIZED ALUMINUM AND UPHOLSTERY, 1934–35.

EDWARD F. CALDWELL & COMPANY

Edward F. Caldwell & Company mastered the art of melding historical styles, including the Colonial Revival, with the modern technology of electricity. The company was founded in New York in 1895 by Edward F. Caldwell and Victor F. von Lossberg. In business until 1959, the firm, which had its own foundry, designed not only light fixtures, but also custom-made metal gates. The firm's significant commissions in New York City included the residence of J. P. Morgan, the New York Public Library, Radio City Music Hall, and the Bank of Manhattan at 40 Wall Street.

LIGHT FIXTURES FROM EDWARD F. CALDWELL & COMPANY CATALOGUE WITH FIXTURE FOR
40 WALL STREET AT RIGHT, 1930.

LIGHT FIXTURE ATTRIBUTED TO EDWARD F. CALDWELL & COMPANY
IN THE LOBBY OF THE MUSEUM OF THE CITY OF NEW YORK, METAL AND GLASS, 1932.

TIFFANY & CO.

Tiffany & Co., an important designer and manufacturer of Colonial Revival objects since as early as the 1870s, launched an especially notable collaboration around World War I with the Metropolitan Museum of Art to create accurate reproductions of Colonial-era silver. These reproductions were based on the museum's collection donated by Judge A. T. Clearwater, whose silver collection was among the first to be given to a museum, thereby elevating the status of such early American artifacts. Tiffany silversmiths painstakingly researched and measured each original intended for reproduction. Full-scale drawings and plaster casts were produced, as were photographs. To give the reproductions an aura of authenticity and pedigree, each was stamped not only with the Tiffany name, but also with the note "Original in the Clearwater Collection, Metropolitan Museum of Art" and information on the original maker, from Paul Revere to Peter van Dyck.

In later decades, responding to consumers who wanted silverware that could fit within simpler interiors, Tiffany created new wares. These products were praised by numerous journalists. "What is true of architecture is true of everything, from skyscrapers to Ernest Hemingway," noted Augusta Owen Patterson in *Town & Country* magazine in 1932. Tiffany's works, she noted, "are quiet, mannerly pieces of solid virtues which can be used with decorum in a room which achieves purity through the sensitive use of receding planes, or in a room which is content to rest on the accomplishments of the English Georgian period."[4]

JUDGE A. T. CLEARWATER'S SILVER COLLECTION AS INSTALLED AT METROPOLITAN MUSEUM OF ART, 1924.

TEAPOT MANUFACTURED BY TIFFANY & CO., SILVER AND IVORY, 1907–25.

REPRODUCTION EDWARD WINSLOW CHOCOLATE POT AND OTHER SERVING PIECES,
MANUFACTURED BY TIFFANY & CO., 1907-1938.

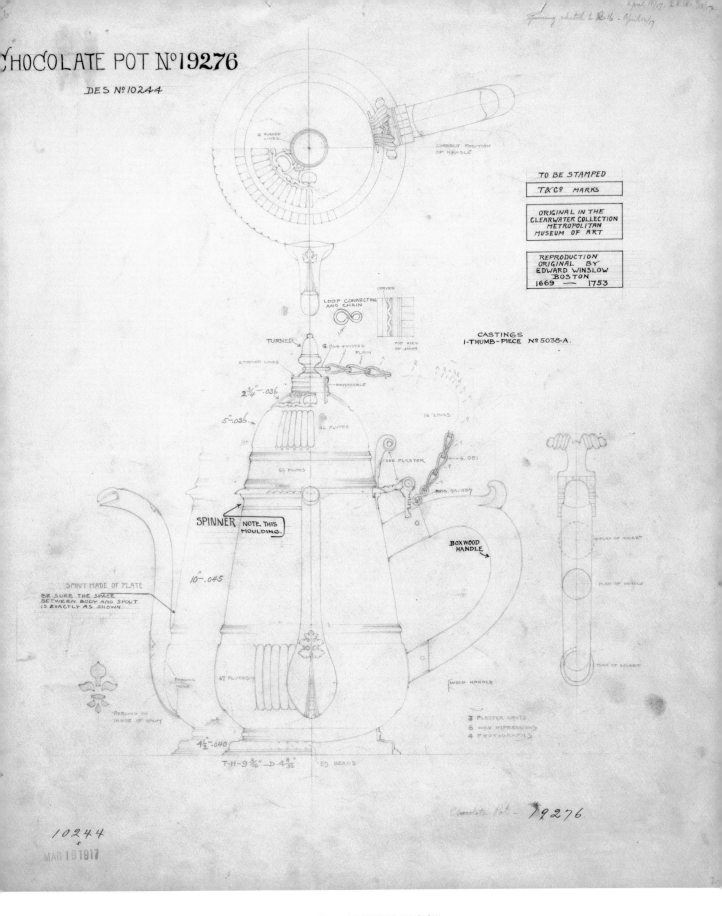

DRAWING FOR TIFFANY & CO. REPRODUCTION OF EDWARD WINSLOW
CHOCOLATE POT, C. 1918.

SIX-PIECE TEA AND COFFEE SERVICE WITH TRAY MANUFACTURED BY TIFFANY & CO.,
STERLING SILVER, 1915–19.

Around 1910, new independent silversmith shops opened across America, some started by
workers who had been laid off from large silver companies, such as the Gorham Manufacturing
Company, in the financial panic of 1907. Some of these shops began producing silverware
that evoked the hand-wrought metalwork of preindustrial America. As this work became
increasingly popular, larger companies took note. In the years around World War I, Tiffany & Co.
introduced its high-quality, limited-production "Special Hand Work" line. This tea and coffee
service is an example. Its design looks back to late-eighteenth-century versions with contours
more gently modeled than its precedents.

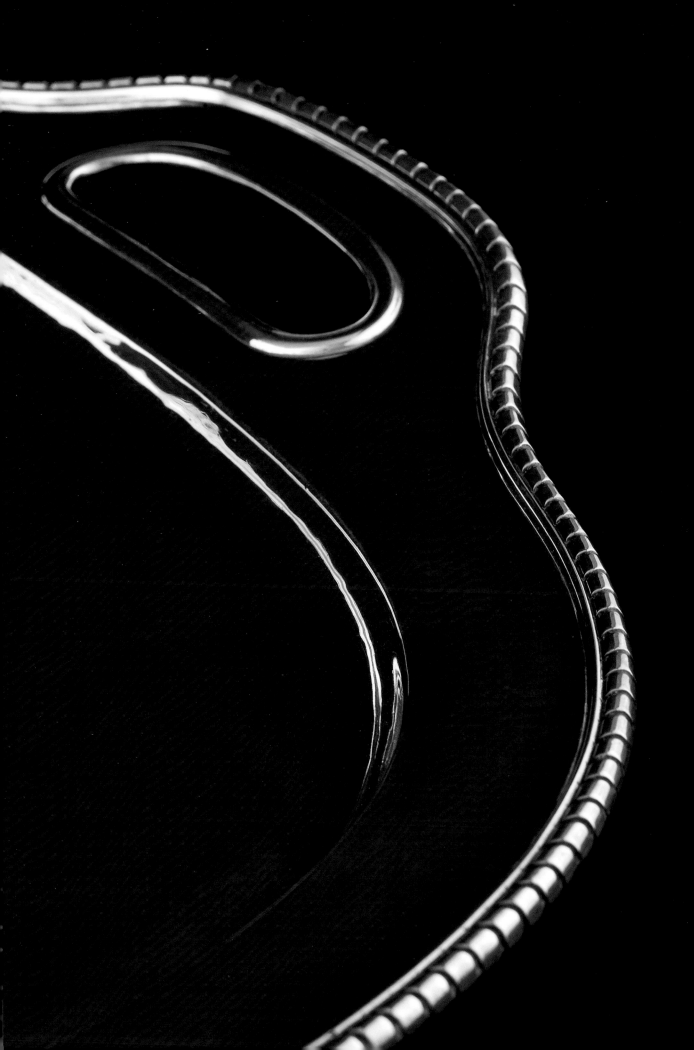

BLACK, STARR & FROST

Black, Starr & Frost traces its roots to 1810. In that year, Erastus Barton and Frederick Marquand opened Marquand and Barton near New York's Maiden Lane. In 1929 Black, Starr & Frost, a noted manufacturer of jewelry and silver with a New York flagship store, merged with Gorham's New York retail operation to create Black, Starr & Frost-Gorham, Inc.

GOLD COFFEE SERVICE FOR TWELVE WITH SALVER MANUFACTURED BY BLACK, STARR & FROST-GORHAM, INC., 1936.

RUSSEL WRIGHT

Although best known for his Depression-era dinnerware in streamlined shapes and solid colors, Russel Wright referred to Colonial Revival forms and rhetoric throughout his career. At its start around 1930, Wright designed objects in traditional pewter and sterling silver. But as the Depression deepened, he created his first popular success—a line of tableware in brushed aluminum that replicated the finish of pewter at much lower cost. "Russel Wright," his sales agent Mary Ryan announced around 1933, "is a modern Paul Revere."[5] A few years later, Russel and his wife, Mary, introduced American Modern furniture, which, according to its manufacturer, Conant Ball, "is the present-day continuation of Colonial American furniture. Built in maple, the wood of our forefathers, it is designed to express in the 20th century manner, the simplicity and frank construction of American Colonial furnitutre."[6]

PEWTER SALT AND PEPPER HOLDERS, DESIGNED BY RUSSEL WRIGHT, 1930.

MAPLE AMERICAN MODERN FURNITURE, C.1935.

ARTHUR TODHUNTER

Although Arthur Todhunter, a British immigrant, initially set up a shop
in New York to sell salvaged architectural elements such as paneling
and fireplaces from England, by the second decade of the twentieth
century he produced reproductions of fine metalwork, including
architectural hardware.

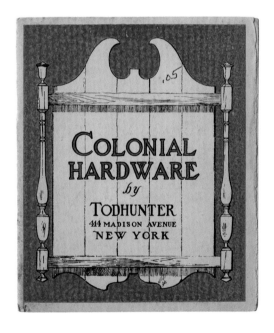 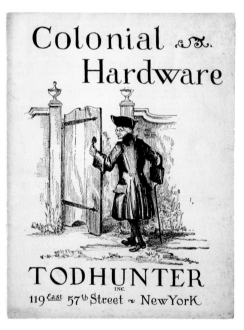

COLONIAL HARDWARE BROCHURE, C.1930.

COLONIAL HARDWARE BROCHURE, 1926 (ABOVE RIGHT AND OPPOSITE).

COLONIAL HARDWARE

HAND wrought period hardware is an investment paying big dividends in both service and satisfaction, and in addition, its use considerably enhances the value of your property. It has been graphically described as "staunch and as full of character as a Pilgrim Father, with a similar austerity which time has made picturesque."

Hand wrought hinges, thumb latches, shutter hooks, etc., contribute in no small measure to the individuality and distinctive appearance of the home and no other hardware is as effective for the Colonial or Early English house.

The interest of hand wrought hardware, particularly the Colonial on account of its simplicity, lies not only in the design, but also in the character of the workmanship and surface texture.

This important feature, however, cannot unfortunately be indicated in a catalogue.

Our hardware is not stamped out or trip hammered, but is forged in the old manner by skilled smiths thoroughly familiar with the early Colonial metalwork, reproducing the original pieces with a fidelity which makes it hardly possible to distinguish the new from the old.

We can now supply these authentic reproductions of early craftsmanship at practically the same cost as stock hardware and you can obtain it with equal facility—*it is not expensive.*

All pieces are put through a process to make them rust resisting and black finished, and are supplied with the necessary hand hammered head screws. On special order it can be supplied half polished or in cast brass in antique finish.

This catalogue has been arranged so that selections for an entire house may very easily be made by reference to the index below. Essential sizes or descriptions not given under the illustrations, will be found on the accompanying price list. Being hand work, slight variations may be found in sizes given.

INDEX

Exterior Doors	Page 3	Casements	Page 8
Dutch Doors	" 4	Shutters	" 9
Cupboards	" 5	Garage	" 10
Interior Doors	" 6	Gates	" 11
French Doors	" 7	Sundry Metalwork	" 12

EXTERIOR DOORS

3135 Large brass knob 3" diameter, for use as door pull, with 2½" stud. (3135A—Same, 2½", 3135B—2", 3135C—1¾" with 5/16 spindle.)
3142‡ Hinge plate, 22" x 2" wide at butt.
3143‡ Hinge plate, 22" x 2" wide at butt.
3145* Thumb latch, 2¾" x 11".
3162 Thumb turn, with 5/16" spindle.
3172* Thumb latch, 3¼" x 12½".
3193 ‡ Box lock, 7¼" x 4¼", face to center of keyhole 2¾", to hub 5⅛", strike 1" wide, with 2" solid knob and 5/16" straight spindle. All brass or antique steel with brass knob. State whether for right or left hand (*illustration is right hand*).
3194 ‡ Solid 2" knob with rose and 5/16" straight spindle. Brass or antique steel.
3195 Heavy covered escutcheon for standard bit-key, 1" x 2⅛". Brass or antique steel.
3202* Thumb latch 4" x 15½".
3209 Cover for 1¼" lock cylinder.
3211* Cast brass thumb latch, 2¼" x 8¾".
7818 Brass letter box slot, 7" x 2½", with concealed bolts for fastening, including brass frame for slot on inside of door.

*To operate a cylinder lock, a thumb latch handle is used on each side of door, with cylinder cover 3209 outside and thumb turn 3162 to throw dead bolt, on inside. We can also supply lock with black front and cylinder, to match hardware. When not used to operate a lock, a 7" latch bar, of type shown for interior doors, is used on inside.

‡We can supply stock butts in black finish for use with these plates. ‡ Also made smaller, see page 6.

Please give thickness of doors

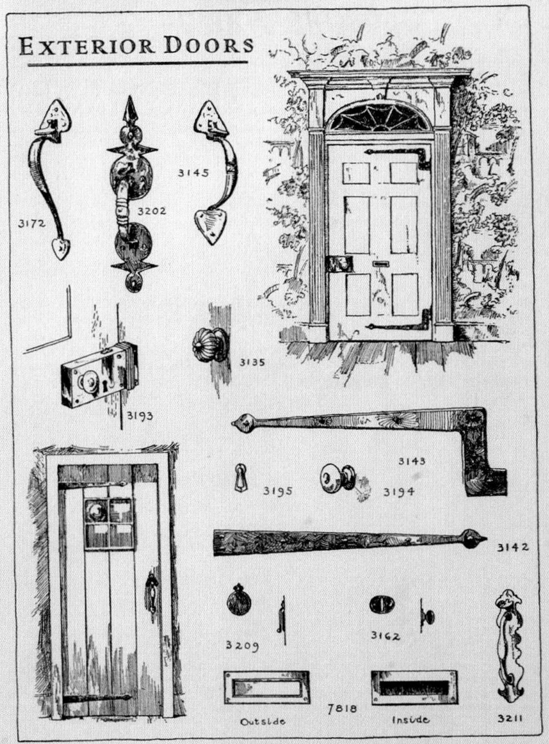

EXTERIOR DOORS
3172
3202
3145
3135
3193
3143
3195
3194
3142
3209
3162
Outside
7818
Inside
3211

For description of above see opposite page.

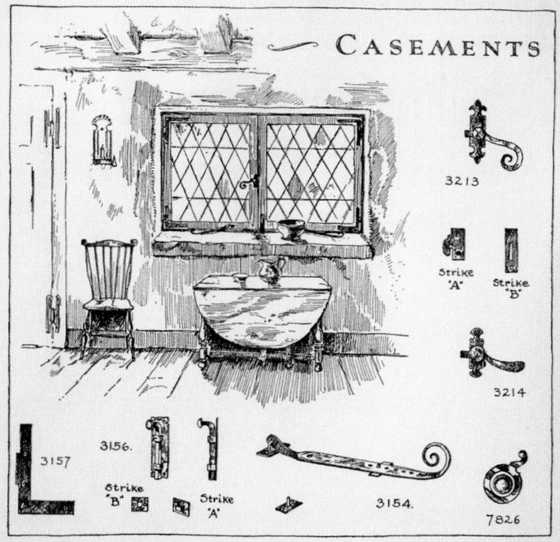

CASEMENTS
3213
Strike "A"
Strike "B"
3214
3157
3156.
Strike "B"
Strike "A"
3154.
7826

3154 Casement adjuster, 12¾" long.
3156 Bolt, back plate 1" x 3½", brass knob. *Please state if trim is flush or otherwise.*
3157 Hinge plate 4" x 6". We can supply stock butts in black finish for use with these.
3213† Lever handle fastener, 4" from center of hub, escutcheon 1" x 3¾".
3214† Lever handle fastener, 4" from center of hub, escutcheon 1⅛" x 3¼".
7826 Brass pull for electric bell, 2½" diameter.

†Please give hand required (*is right hand as shown,*) and if trim on center mullion (if any) is flush or otherwise.

NOTES

Any hinge plate can be supplied to special order, made with butt as a complete hinge.

Many of these designs are suitable made in brass, which can be supplied on special order,

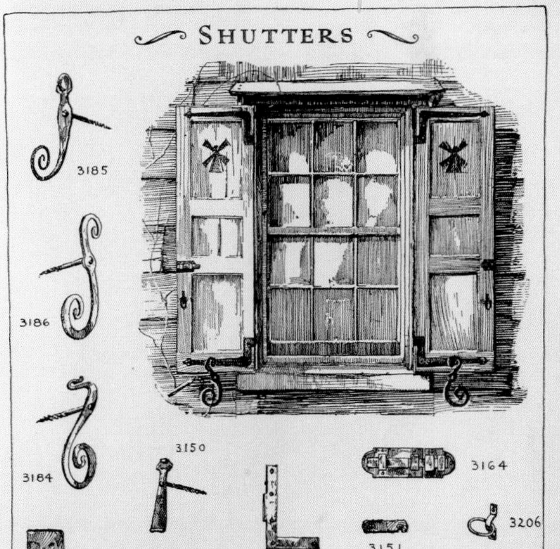

SHUTTERS
3185
3186
3184
3150
3164
3206
3151
3141
3157
3140

3140‡ Hinge plate, 14" x 1¾" at butt.
3141‡ Hinge plate, 14" x 2" at butt.
3150 Hold back, length 6", on 5" lag.
3151 Latch, 3½" long.
3157‡ Hinge plate, 4" x 6".
3164 Bolt, 4⅝" x 2", strike 2¼" long. (3164A—same 2⅞" x 1⅜" strike 1⅛" long).
3184* Hold back, length 7", mounted on 5" lag screw.
3185 Hold back, length 7", mounted on 5" lag.
3186* Hold back length 9¼", (3186A—same 6½" long) mounted on 5" lag screw.
3206 Ring pulls, 2½" diameter.

‡For use with stock butt. *Nos. 3184 and 3186 are reversible so as to make pairs.

ARCHITECTS' TEA SERVICE

During the Great Depression, in an effort to provide work for unemployed architects and draftsmen and raise money for relief to architects in need, the Women's Division of the Architects' Emergency Committee in New York, composed of fourteen members of the architectural profession, pursued a number of projects. One of the committee's most successful fund-raising efforts was the production by the Lenox Company of five thousand so-called Architects' Tea Services. Colonial in design and decorated with drawings of historic American buildings, each basic set comprised a teapot, cream pitcher, sugar bowl, and six cups and saucers. The committee sold the tea services through thirty-five dollar subscriptions. Members of the committee who helped organize the effort included the etiquette arbiter Emily Post and the architect William Lawrence Bottomley.

ARCHITECTS' TEA SERVICE, MANUFACTURED BY LENOX COMPANY,
TRENTON, NEW JERSEY, PORCELAIN, 1933.

BLOOMINGDALE'S OLD NEW YORK SERIES

Bloomingdale's Old New York dishes featured historic views of sites in the city, such as Niblo's Garden, Fraunces Tavern, Old Washington Market, and the Croton Reservoir.

EARTHENWARE PLATES MANUFACTURED BY WILLIAM ADAMS & SONS OF ENGLAND
FOR BLOOMINGDALE'S DEPARTMENT STORE, 1914–40, DEPICTING, BROAD STREET (ABOVE)
AND FRAUNCES TAVERN (RIGHT).

STEUBEN GLASS

In 1933 Arthur Amory Houghton Jr., a twenty-seven-year-old member of the family that controlled Corning Glass Works, decided to catapult the company's financially failing Steuben Division—later renamed Steuben Glass—into the realm of contemporary design. Using a new, unusually pure lead crystal, Steuben designers and glassmakers created objects from candlesticks to cocktail glasses and cigarette boxes that were as aesthetically malleable as glass itself. During the 1930s, Steuben designs, presented in its various chic Manhattan shops, ranged from undecorated bowls to faceted Art Deco vases and new glass interpretations of eighteenth-century models. The latter included F. B. Sellew's teardrop candlesticks (with teardrop-shaped air bubbles trapped within their columns) to John Gates's 1939 cream pitcher with lavish curlicues.

GLASS BALUSTER CANDLESTICKS WITH DOMED FEET DESIGNED BY F. B. SELLEW
FOR STEUBEN, 1937.

GLASS CREAM PITCHER DESIGNED BY JOHN MONTEITH GATES FOR STEUBEN, 1939.

COLONIAL BIBLES & BALLYHOO

PUBLICATIONS, EXHIBITIONS, AND STAGE-SET ARCHITECTURE

Photograph by Trowbridge

DETAIL OF DOORWAY AND PEDIMENT LEADING FROM ENTRANCE
HALL TO THE SMALL SITTING ROOM, MOUNT VERNON,
FAIRFAX COUNTY, VIRGINIA

81

PUBLICATIONS

COLONIAL FURNITURE IN AMERICA

Throughout the first half of the twentieth century, books and magazines were the primary means for promulgating the revival of early American decorative arts. *Colonial Furniture in America*, first published in 1901, was a pioneering historical study issued in numerous editions. Its author, Luke Vincent Lockwood, was a collector and scholar who would serve as an advisor on the Hudson-Fulton exhibition at the Metropolitan Museum of Art in 1909, and later helped to organize period rooms at the Brooklyn Museum and the Museum of the City of New York.

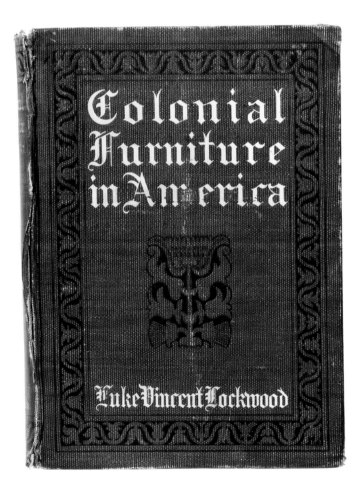

LUKE VINCENT LOCKWOOD, *COLONIAL FURNITURE IN AMERICA*, PUBLISHED BY CHARLES SCRIBNER'S SONS, NEW YORK, 1913 EDITION.

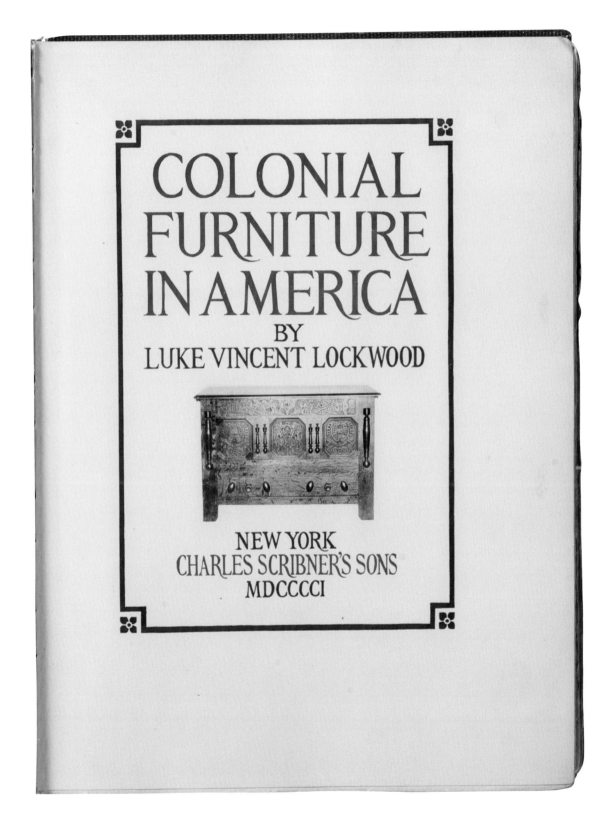

VANITY FAIR, JULY 1926

Celebrating the 150th anniversary of the signing of the Declaration of Independence, *Vanity Fair* magazine devoted an entire issue to "trace back," its editorial claimed, "and to consider the state of our national culture in 1776." Through a series of paired drawings, the magazine compared Colonial customs with those of present-day New York, the city of "the motor car, the radio, the tabloid newspaper, shorts skirts, comic strips, and prohibition."[1]

ADVERTISEMENT FOR SAKS FIFTH AVENUE.

VANITY FAIR, JULY 1926.

In This Special Number:

**Sherwood Anderson · Robert C. Benchley · Heywood Broun · Miguel Covarrubias
Theodore Dreiser · Walter Prichard Eaton · Corey Ford · Milt Gross
George Jean Nathan · Jim Tully · A. B. Walkley · Alexander Woollcott**

JULY, 1926   © *The* CONDÉ NAST PUBLICATIONS, *Inc.*   35 CTS · $3.50 A YEAR

"1776—COURTSHIP THEN AND NOW—1926," DRAWING BY WILLIAM BOLIN.

GREAT GEORGIAN HOUSES OF AMERICA

Scholarly books codified the great houses of the period and provided
measured drawings for contemporary architects to follow. Like the
Architects' Tea Service, this book was a product of the Architects'
Emergency Committee in New York to help unemployed architects.
The year this book was published, the committee hired architects
to create scale models of historic New York buildings, including the
original Federal Hall, Hamilton Grange, and Fraunces Tavern.
The models were displayed at Rockefeller Center.

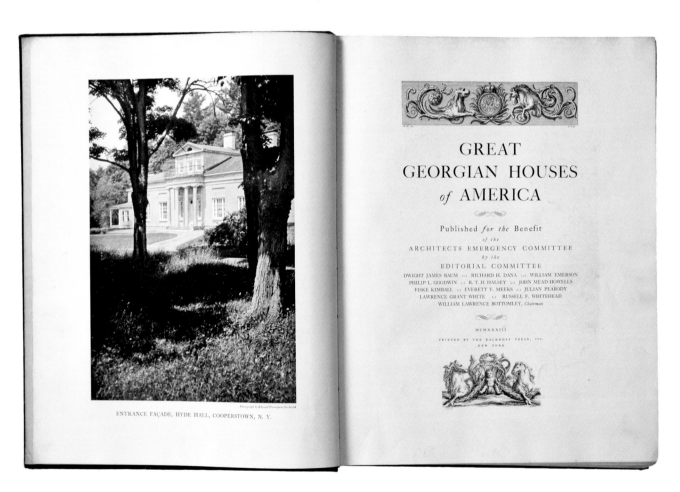

ENTRANCE FAÇADE, HYDE HALL, COOPERSTOWN, N. Y.

WILLIAM LAWRENCE BOTTOMLEY, EDITOR, *GREAT GEORGIAN HOUSES OF AMERICA*,
PUBLISHED BY THE KALKHOFF PRESS, 1933.

THE MAGAZINE ANTIQUES

The Magazine Antiques was pivotal in both stimulating interest in the nation's Colonial past and promoting Colonial Revival design. Advertisements featuring dealers of Colonial furnishings, as well as manufacturers of Colonial Revival reproductions, augmented editorial coverage.

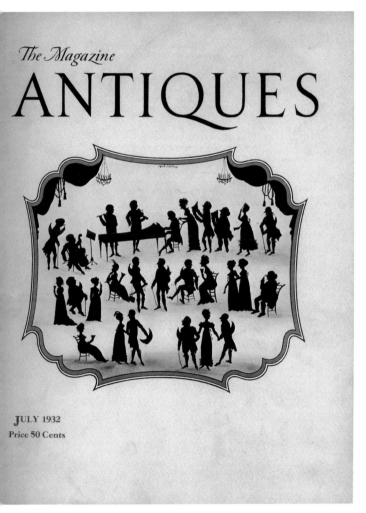

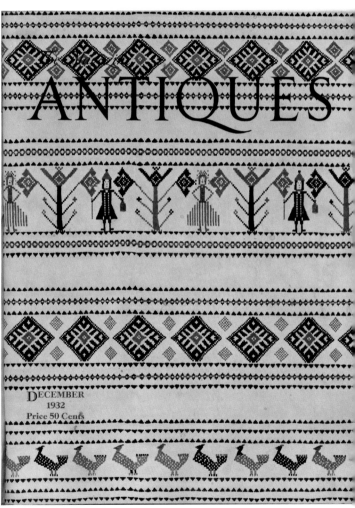

THE MAGAZINE ANTIQUES, JULY 1932.

THE MAGAZINE ANTIQUES, DECEMBER 1932.

EXHIBITIONS AND STAGE-SET ARCHITECTURE

HUDSON-FULTON CELEBRATION, 1909

The elaborately staged Hudson-Fulton Celebration was held in New York City from September 25 to October 9, 1909, commemorating both the tercentennial of Henry Hudson's third and most-documented voyage and the centennial of the first successful commercial operation of Robert Fulton's newly invented steamboat (the passage of the *Clermont* on the Hudson River). A commission whose members included Andrew Carnegie and J. P. Morgan organized the celebration, which was four years in the making. It served not only to commemorate specific historic events, but also to catalyze interest in New York's past and express its growing power as a world-class city.

Unprecedented in local history in terms of its expense and popularity, the celebration exerted an effect beyond the duration of fifteen days in several significant ways. In keeping with the Progressive Movement's focus on education, the Hudson-Fulton Celebration Commission utilized aspects of their activities, including the event's Historical Parade and Children's Festival, as well as ancillary programs in schools and settlement houses, as a way of educating a diverse population about their city's heritage and traditions. The celebration, in fact, nearly coincided with the height of immigration from Eastern and Southern Europe, which peaked at one million people in 1907. The celebration also included a loan exhibition of American decorative arts at the Metropolitan Museum of Art that proved seminal in that institution's evolution.

PROGRAM FROM HUDSON-FULTON CELEBRATION, 1909.

COMMEMORATIVE SPOON FROM HUDSON-FULTON CELEBRATION, TIFFANY & CO., 1909.

THE METROPOLITAN MUSEUM OF ART
AMERICAN WING, 1924

The Metropolitan Museum's establishment of its American Wing marked a pivotal moment in the increasing recognition of American decorative arts, including both Colonial-era objects and Colonial Revival style objects, as aesthetically significant and worthy of collection. From nearly its inception in 1870, the museum had exhibited and collected American art, but it was not until 1909, in conjunction with the landmark Hudson-Fulton Celebration, that the museum mounted a loan exhibition of American paintings and decorative art objects from the Colonial and early Republican periods in an effort, as museum president Robert W. de Forest later stated, "to test out the question whether American domestic art was worthy of a place in an art museum."[2] In 1910 the museum adopted a focus on American decorative art objects made prior to 1815 and purchased H. Eugene Bolles's furniture collection, which served as the core of an autonomous American Wing.

The museum's American Wing, designed by the architect Grosvenor Atterbury, who had previously worked on the restoration of New York's early-nineteenth-century City Hall, opened in 1924. The American Wing's first curator, R. T. Haines Halsey, asserted that the displays would counter "the influx of foreign ideas utterly at variance with those held by the men who gave us the Republic" by presenting "traditions so dear to us and so invaluable in the Americanization of many of our people, to whom much of our history is little known."[3] The wing's compact rooms, well suited to the display of furniture and domestic objects, stood in marked contrast to the grandeur of the classical galleries at the museum.

MAIN SECOND-FLOOR GALLERY, AMERICAN WING, THE METROPOLITAN MUSEUM OF ART, 1924.

The contemporary cornice and trim in this room were modeled after elements of a mantelpiece in the Beekman House (1763), located in New York City's Turtle Bay neighborhood and once considered one of the city's most imposing residences.

COVER IMAGE OF THE *BULLETIN* ANNOUNCING THE OPENING OF THE AMERICAN WING AT
THE METROPOLITAN MUSEUM OF ART, NEW YORK CITY, NOVEMBER 1924.

OLD NEW YORK, MUSEUM OF THE CITY OF NEW YORK, 1926

Billed as "the first of its kind ever attempted in this city," this exhibition was presented during the first week of November 1926 in the Fine Arts Building on West 57th Street. Then located in Gracie Mansion, the Museum of the City of New York organized the show, which brought together heirlooms lent by numerous first families of New York. The exhibition was conceived not only to offer a fascinating picture of the city's past, but also to convince New Yorkers "how swiftly the panorama of New York life is changing," a member of the committee noted, "and the importance of preserving now . . . the objects we are using today."[4]

OLD NEW YORK, 1926.

GIRL SCOUTS LOAN EXHIBITION, 1929

Organized by New York collector Louis Guerineau Myers and conceived by his wife as a way to raise funds for the National Council of Girl Scouts, the *Girl Scouts Loan Exhibition* of American antiques was held at the galleries of the American Art Association from September 25 to October 9, 1929. Drawn from personal collections and institutions such as the Museum of the City of New York, the exhibition culminated the decade in which collectors and museums legitimized the aesthetic significance of American antiques.

DUNCAN PHYFE FURNITURE EXHIBITED AT THE *GIRL SCOUTS LOAN EXHIBITION*, 1929.

GEORGE WASHINGTON BICENTENNIAL, 1932

By the Great Depression, New York City rode a pendulum of opposing forces. The city had just completed a wholesale transformation of itself from a low-lying harbor town, whose highest peaks were church steeples, to a modern metropolis, with a skyline of corporate skyscrapers was recognizable the world over. Yet surprisingly, in the face of this new status, many significant events looked not to the city's future but to its past. The social and economic upheavals of the time, such as immigration, depression, and war, further spurred people's desire for tradition. In 1932 the bicentennial of George Washington's birth was celebrated in the spectacular Beaux-Arts ball at the Waldorf Astoria Hotel, with the city's leading figures in Colonial-style dresses available from department stores. In the spring, major pageants celebrated the bicentennial with replicas of Federal Hall in Bryant Park, dedicated by Mayor Jimmy Walker, and of Mount Vernon in Prospect Park. The Federal Hall replica was designed by Joseph H. Freedlander, and the Mount Vernon replica by Charles K. Bryant; Sears, Roebuck & Company served as the contractors for both structures. The interiors of the Mount Vernon re-creation contained furniture and objects lent by the Metropolitan Museum of Art and the Brooklyn Museum, as well as dealers Israel Sack and Ginsburg and Levy. Manufacturers in Grand Rapids, Michigan, provided reproduction furniture.

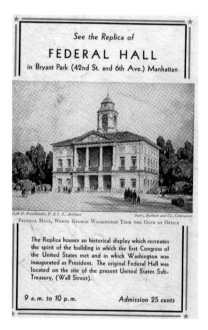

FRONT COVER OF *OFFICIAL HANDBOOK OF THE REPLICA OF MOUNT VERNON*, 1932.

BACK COVER OF *OFFICIAL HANDBOOK OF THE REPLICA OF MOUNT VERNON*, SHOWING THE REPLICA OF FEDERAL HALL IN BRYANT PARK, 1932.

ADVERTISEMENT FOR B. ALTMAN & COMPANY, *NEW YORK TIMES*, JANUARY 7, 1932.

The copy for this advertisement read: "If you're going to the Beaux-Arts Ball on the twenty-second, let us show you the authentic Colonial costumes made of Celanese Fabrics."

IMAGE FROM HELEN JOHNSON KEYES, "FOR WASHINGTON BICENTENARY PARTIES," *CHRISTIAN SCIENCE MONITOR*, FEBRUARY 3, 1932.

SAMUEL MCINTIRE ROOM AT THE ARNOLD CONSTABLE COLONIAL EXHIBITION, 1932

Since the end of the nineteenth century, New York City stores erected full-scale rooms and even houses as temporary settings in which to display and sell furniture. In some cases, antiques were presented to underscore the historical pedigree of contemporary furniture for sale in the store, while in other cases examples of the store's for-sale historicist furnishings were featured. In conjunction with the George Washington Bicentennial, New York department store Arnold Constable presented its Colonial Exhibition, which featured a room taken from a house in Salem, Massachusetts. The house was built by woodcarver, architect, and builder Samuel McIntire. The *Colonial Exhibition* also involved the efforts of collector and dealer Israel Sack, who lent Colonial-era objects, and Nancy McClelland, who designed a scenic wallpaper that, according to the *New York Times*, "has much of the spirit of the old pictorial wall coverings."[5]

WALTER RENDELL STOREY, "RICH VARIETY FOUND IN COLONIAL ROOMS," WITH A PHOTOGRAPH SHOWING A SCENIC WALLPAPER DESIGNED BY NANCY MCCLELLAND, *NEW YORK TIMES*, MARCH 13, 1932.

RICH VARIETY FOUND IN COLONIAL ROOMS

Exhibits of Interiors Show the Effect of Vogues and Needs of the Period

A Samuel McIntire Room Shown by Flayderman at the Arnold Constable Colonial Exhibition.

By WALTER RENDELL STOREY

THE many historical exhibitions inspired by the Washington bicentennial are recreating for the antiquarian and the decorator vivid details of everyday Colonial life. Entire rooms have been constructed and furnished with appropriate antiques, and displays of costumes and pictures of old-time scenes aid in the visualization of former days.

A better understanding of Colonial life in America is eradicating several popular misconceptions, as, for example, the belief that homes in those early days were furnished strictly in one style. A Colonial household just after the Revolution may have had many pieces in the straight, simple-lined Sheraton style then in vogue, but it may have possessed also a Chippendale chair or sofa in the earlier rococo style of curves and profuse carving, or even a Queen Anne wing chair.

Fine old furniture was not discarded then any more than now; a useful piece was re-upholstered or had its wood refinished to give it the effect of newness. The home of a newly wedded couple might be furnished in the latest fashion, but later, perhaps, when an heirloom was bequeathed to the family, the older piece would be incorporated with the newer furniture.

A home in a city where good craftsmen were available and imported articles could be easily obtained would follow the vogues much more closely than would a country mansion further removed from the sources of supply. A farm home often acquired a more native flavor through its home-made chairs and hooked rugs, woven coverlets, and andirons and hardware wrought by the village blacksmith than did the city establishments where everything was made either by expert craftsmen or ordered from London and Paris.

Evidences of these interesting variations of Colonial furnishings may be observed in two recently opened exhibitions—one at Arnold Constable's, and the other at the Newark Museum.

THE Arnold Constable display was organized under the direction of Monroe Douglas Robinson, aided by a committee of prominent men and women and the New York City Board of Education. Rare documents, prints, paintings and antique furnishings recreate a graphic picture of Washington's time.

A feature of this exhibition is a room taken from a house in Salem,

Mass., built by Samuel McIntire, the famous wood carver, architect and builder of a century and a half ago. The carved doorways, with overdoor panels of garlands and classic figures painted in an old ivory hue, and the fine carved mantel in the same restrained classic style are exceptional examples of room decoration. The room, which is exhibited through the courtesy of the House of Flayderman, as is also the furniture, is further enriched by a colorful wallpaper depicting classic scenes, which was printed in Paris by Dufour about 1830. In keeping with the custom of the time when the house was built, a low wainscoting provides a chair rail and a base for the scenic wallpaper, which extends upward to a finely carved cornice molding.

Samuel McIntire not only created beautiful interior woodwork, but he is now credited with making and carving fine mahogany furniture. The room at Arnold Constable's is furnished with pieces attributed to him, all of them bearing the star-punched background which he characteristically used for his carvings. A long sofa with gracefully curving ends has this detail in the panel on the top of the back,

and a lady's dressing table and a sewing table are similarly marked. These pieces are all in the classic, restrained Sheraton style.

In pleasing contrast with the other mahogany furniture is a curly satinwood secretary attributed to John Seymour, the Boston cabinetmaker, noted for his delicate designs and fine inlay. A peculiarity of Seymour, which aids in the identification of this piece, is that he always painted the interiors of the shelves and cubbyholes a sky blue. Hooked rugs cover the floor of this McIntire-built room.

A BEDROOM ensemble displays a four-poster McIntire bed with the rare feature of a carved wood canopy on which, in small central panels, appear the typical McIntire baskets of fruits and flowers. This also is exhibited by the House of Flayderman.

The other furniture in the bedroom is displayed through the courtesy of Israel Sack. A diversity of styles is suggested here in the dignified walnut chest-on-chest that dates from about the middle of the eighteenth century and the Martha Washington chair with its upholstered back and seat and grace-

fully curved supports for the wooden arms, in vogue about 1790 and later. A Chippendale lowboy, with ball and claw feet and a shell-ornamented panel, dating from the midcentury, associates with a Curtis clock which was made around 1800. Antique toile de Jouy, or French printed chintz, designed by J. B. Huet in 1783 and lent by Elinor Merrell, drapes the windows.

A dining-room group, with the furniture and a beautifully carved pine mantel lent by Israel Sack, provides a setting for silver and china. A long mahogany table with square, tapering legs inlaid with satinwood is laid with a Lowestoft dinner set in brown and gold, shown through the courtesy of D. A. Bernstein; a feature of the set is a huge soup tureen with its cover.

Some of the silver that once belonged to General Washington is displayed on the Sheraton sideboard. Like the furniture, the silverware shows various styles of designs, ranging from the simple coffee pot made by a Philadelphia silversmith, in which the lines of the piece are its greatest charm, to the heavily engraved and ornamented pieces in the Georgian style of the day. The Washington silver is lent

by Mrs. Billing Lee and Mrs. Robert E. Lee. A Bilbao mirror lavishly carved and gilded, with an inlay of yellow marble, adds to the interest of the ensemble. This rare type of mirror was found in wealthy homes in Colonial seaports and is supposed to have been imported from Portugal.

Taking up a large part of a long wall in the exhibition room is a scenic wallpaper recently designed by Nancy McClelland, which has much of the spirit of the old pictorial wall coverings. In a panorama are depicted incidents in the inauguration of Washington as President, including his arrival at Fulton Wharf in New York, the parade along the streets, his taking of the oath on the balcony of the Federal Building and his later visit to St. Paul's Chapel.

*　*　*

THE Colonial Life Exhibition at the Newark Museum, besides including documents and articles of local historical interest, presents antique household furnishings and farm implements and a complete, old-fashioned kitchen. While much fine workmanship is displayed, there are also many examples of home-made craft such as were found in every farmhouse and village dwelling. Here, as in the more pretentious homes of the Colonial era, articles in both old and new styles are to be found together.

Thus in Colonial days and up into the first decades of the nineteenth century a hand-woven blue coverlet made from wool grown, spun and dyed by the household, might associate with printed cotton bed draperies from a factory; or a "betty" lamp or a candlestick wrought by the village blacksmith would serve in the kitchen, while the "best" room would have the latest pattern of glass or pewter whale-oil lamp. Red and yellow slip ware were made and used in the Colonies at the same time that the more sophisticated Staffordshire, Liverpool and Lowestoft wares of England were being introduced.

The Colonial kitchen, as is illustrated by the one in the exhibition, was not only a place where meals were cooked but the scene of many household activities. Here yarn was spun for cloth and later dyed in huge iron kettles hung on the

(Continued on Page 17)

A Colonial Kitchen Exhibited at the Newark Museum.

Photo Courtesy Newark Museum.

AMERICA'S LITTLE HOUSE

Developed by the New York chapter of Better Homes in America, a professional organization representing the housing industry, in association with the Columbia Broadcasting System, America's Little House was a model home designed by Roger H. Bullard and Clifford C. Windehack. Constructed for eight thousand dollars, the eight-room house was intended to serve the needs of a family of average income. During its year of operation from the fall of 1934 until the fall of 1935, the house, located amidst tall buildings in midtown Manhattan, received some 165,000 visitors, including First Lady Eleanor Roosevelt, who dedicated its black marble hearthstone. Referring to the house, author Pearl Buck noted, "Drudgery is gone from between these walls, although there are not servants in the house. Labor is incredibly lightened, and beauty of living seems made almost inevitable. Above it all stand the tall towers of New York, the towers were so much business and pleasure are carried on. But the little house stands unperturbed and unfrightened."[6]

The Better Homes in America organization participated in the Better Homes Movement, a national campaign initiated in 1922 to foster home ownership, modernization, improvement, and decoration. When the Better Homes Movement was launched by President Warren G. Harding and Secretary of Commerce Herbert Hoover, a replica of the Colonial Long Island house of John Howard Payne, songwriter of "Home! Sweet Home!," was built on the White House lawn. Given the organization's national agenda, it was not surprising that the Colonial Revival was the preferred style of its various demonstration houses.

AMERICA'S LITTLE HOUSE, PARK AVENUE AND EAST 39TH STREET, NEW YORK CITY.
PHOTOGRAPH BY RICHARD AVERILL SMITH.

Bert Lawson

POSTCARD OF AMERICA'S LITTLE HOUSE.
PHOTOGRAPH BY BERT LAWSON.

POSTCARD OF INTERIOR OF AMERICA'S LITTLE HOUSE.
PHOTOGRAPH BY RICHARD AVERILL SMITH.

NEW HORIZONS IN AMERICAN ART, MUSEUM OF MODERN ART

In the fall of 1936, the Museum of Modern Art presented this exhibition devoted to artists working on the Federal Art Project, which had been established by the federal government to support Depression-era artists. Among the many paintings and prints featured in the show, *New Horizons* also included watercolors by artists sponsored by an FAP program, the Index of American Design. Produced between 1935 and 1942, the Index comprises approximately eighteen thousand watercolor renderings of American decorative arts objects from the Colonial period through the nineteenth century. Such documentation was part of a larger movement that encompassed the Colonial Revival and sought to define American identity.

WATERCOLOR OF CARVER ARMCHAIR BY ANNE GER CREATED FOR THE INDEX OF AMERICAN DESIGN, 1936.

Named after John Carver, the first governor of Plymouth Colony, this type of armchair was typical of those produced in the colony between 1630 and 1670.

NEW YORK WORLD'S FAIR OF 1939/40

The New York World's Fair perfectly captured its moment by looking both forward with optimism, promising in its slogan to "build the world of tomorrow," and backward with pride as a commemoration of the sesquicentennial of George Washington's presidential inauguration in New York, then the nation's capital, in 1789. The cover of an issue of the *New York Times Magazine* devoted to the fair showed James Earle Fraser's monumental sculpture of Washington against the backdrop of the Fair's signature Trylon and Perisphere. In this way, the Colonial past was seamlessly integrated into the nation's future. Similarly, in the Town of Tomorrow, Colonial Revival homes took their place next to futuristic models.

BRONZE MEDAL COMMEMORATING THE 150TH ANNIVERSARY OF GEORGE WASHINGTON'S
INAUGURATION IN NEW YORK CITY, ENGRAVED BY ALBERT N. STEWART, 1939.

COMMEMORATIVE EARTHENWARE PLATES WITH BLUE TRANSFER PRINTED DESIGNS
MANUFACTURED BY WEDGWOOD, C. 1939.

The British company Wedgwood produced these plates with images of pre-twentieth-century
New York sites from the Stadt Huys (state house) in 1676, City Hall in 1791, and Wall Street and
Trinity Church in 1829.

HOUSE NUMBER 6 AT THE TOWN OF TOMORROW, NEW YORK WORLD'S FAIR.
PHOTOGRAPH BY WURTS BROTHERS COMPANY.

TOWN OF TOMORROW BROCHURE, NEW YORK WORLD'S FAIR.

POSTCARD SHOWING COLONIAL REVIVAL STYLE MODEL HOUSES IN THE TOWN
OF TOMORROW AT THE NEW YORK WORLD'S FAIR,
FLUSHING MEADOWS, QUEENS, NEW YORK.

DREAM HOUSE, 1948 AND 1949

This Colonial Revival demonstration house was one of many post–World War II efforts by architects, manufacturers, and professional organizations to define suitable housing for returning GIs and their families. Located on a midtown Manhattan site previously occupied by other model houses, the so-called "Dream House" was part of a fund-raising effort undertaken by the New York Heart Association. A version of the house was offered as first prize in a jingle-writing contest, for which the entrance fee served as a contribution to the association. The house was one of seventy similar model houses built nationwide; all of the houses were inspired by the house described in Eric Hodgins's popular novel, later made into a movie, *Mr. Blandings Builds His Dream House*. In 1948 the Colonial Revival house, built by Johnson Quality Homes, Inc., featured interiors designed by the decorating staff at Macy's; the following years the interiors were redesigned by the interior decorator Patricia Harvey. In both cases, the traditional house incorporated numerous up-to-date labor-saving devices and building materials, including Presti-Glass, a corrugated amalgam of fiberglass and plastic.

FASHION MODEL IN FRONT OF DREAM HOUSE II, FIFTH AVENUE AND 48TH STREET, NEW YORK CITY, 1949.
PHOTOGRAPH BY GENEVIEVE NAYLOR FOR *COSMOPOLITAN* MAGAZINE.

AN
ENDURING
STYLE

COLONIAL REVIVAL TODAY

THE COLONIAL REVIVAL PRODUCED PARTICULARLY ROBUST
architecture and design between the nation's centennial and the advent
of World War II, but it began before 1876 and continues to this day.
Indeed, the movement is perhaps best understood as a series of revivals,
each of which has responded to specific events and main currents—for
example, the centennial, various local and national anniversaries,
immigration, and the Great Depression. Shifting tastes and ideologies
within the architectural and design communities have also played a role.

After World War II, with leading architects' near-exclusive focus
on Modernism, a split developed: Colonial Revival largely disappeared
from the urban scene, while it remained popular, although often watered
down, in the surrounding suburbs. A few individuals and organizations,
however, spoke in alternative voices. Beginning in 1956, Henry Hope
Reed Jr. gave walking tours of New York's classical architecture in an
effort to build a preservationist constituency. In 1959 he wrote the book
The Golden City, in which he unfavorably compared Modernist buildings
to their traditionalist counterparts, and he founded the important
advocacy group Classical America nine years later. (In 2002 this group
joined forces with the Institute of Classical Architecture.) Also in the
1950s, John Barrington Bayley's monumental visionary schemes for New
York City further stimulated interest in classicism, particularly among
practitioners. At the same time, architectural preservation was being
transformed from a specialized interest to a popular one. In 1963 the
destruction of McKim, Mead & White's Pennsylvania Station sparked the
creation of New York City's Landmarks Preservation Commission. The
same year also brought the publication of Robert Venturi's *Complexity
and Contradiction in Architecture* (published by the Museum of Modern
Art), which pointed a young generation toward an inclusive architecture
once again embracing historical reference. While none of these efforts
focused exclusively on Colonial Revival, collectively they fostered an
environment that opened the eyes of architects and designers to the style
as a living tradition.

Allan Greenberg and Robert A. M. Stern were among the
first high-profile architects to reconnect with the rich traditions of the
Colonial Revival. Greenberg's grandly evocative, Mount Vernon–inspired
farmhouse in Connecticut of 1983 garnered broad attention. Three years
later, Stern, who had already been pursuing a variety of classically rooted
architectural styles, hosted a documentary television series, *Pride of Place:
Building the American Dream,* that explored the nation's architectural
heritage and its continued relevance. Recently, Stern's designs for
Villanova Heights, a residential development adjacent to Fieldston in
the Bronx, echo Dwight James Baum's early-twentieth-century Colonial
Revival work in the area.

A younger generation of architects has followed in the footsteps
of Greenberg and Stern. Peter Pennoyer worked at Robert A. M. Stern
Architects before opening his own firm. Pennoyer has also coauthored
a series of books on important American architects working in classical
styles such as Delano & Aldrich. Anne Fairfax and Richard Sammons
established their architectural practice in 1992. Gil P. Schafer III started
his architectural firm, G. P. Schafer Architect, in 2002, having previously
worked for Peter Pennoyer.

While decorative artists and interior designers have consistently
embraced the Colonial Revival, since the 1980s the style has been mined
in particularly inventive—and sometimes humorous and ironic—ways.
Launched with a collection of architect-designed dinnerware in 1984,
New York–based Swid Powell was the brainchild of two alumnae of the
ardently Modernist firm Knoll International, Nan Swid and Addie Powell.
Swid Powell's products reflected the era's diverse architectural trends,
including a historicism that updated, sometimes in a straightforward
manner, sometimes with an ironic twist, the style practiced by prominent
Colonial Revivalists earlier in the century. James Boyd and Anne Reath
have picked up on the wit of these designs in wallpaper by representing
unexpected figures, from Nefertiti to Charles de Gaulle, in silhouette.
Jewelry designer Ted Muehling creates decorative art objects,
collaborating with such manufacturers as Steuben and Nymphenburg.
In 2009 Muehling and seven other fine and decorative artists took part
in a program sponsored by *The Magazine Antiques* and the Shelburne
Museum in Vermont. During a weekend at the museum, the artists
surveyed its vast collections, and each selected one artifact that inspired
them to create a contemporary design. Muehling's chandelier was sparked
by a Colonial-era one in the museum's Stencil House.

Among interior designers now looking to Colonial Revival
for inspiration, three firms stand out for their particularly inventive
approaches. The Dickstein Residence (1999) by William Diamond and
Anthony Baratta is a psychedelic update of Colonial Revival with braided
rugs reminiscent of Wallace Nutting, but here rendered 60 feet long
and colored acid green and shocking pink. Manhattan decorator Jeffrey
Bilhuber's recent renovation of a seventeenth-century Long Island house,
which he uses as a weekend residence and christened Hay Fever, artfully
mixes furnishing and decorative effects from numerous periods, including
the Colonial, while the interiors of Jamie Drake for the late-eighteenth-
century Gracie Mansion constitute a bold essay in the Colonial Revival for
the twenty-first century.

ROBERT A. M. STERN

FLINT HALL AND EDELMAN HALL, HOTCHKISS SCHOOL, LAKEVILLE, CONNECTICUT, 2007.
PHOTOGRAPH BY PETER AARON/ESTO.

VILLANOVA HEIGHTS, RIVERDALE, BRONX, NEW YORK, 2009.
PHOTOGRAPH BY CHRIS KENDALL.

ALLAN GREENBERG

FARMHOUSE IN CONNECTICUT, 1983.
PHOTOGRAPH BY PETER MAUSS/ESTO.

FARMHOUSE IN CONNECTICUT, 1983.
PHOTOGRAPHS BY PETER MAUSS/ESTO.

ANNE FAIRFAX AND RICHARD SAMMONS

CARRIAGE HOUSE AND STUDIO, WEST FOURTH STREET BETWEEN BARROW AND
MORTON STREETS, NEW YORK CITY, 2007. INTERIOR DESIGNED BY ANNE FAIRFAX
AND MARINA KILLERY.
PHOTOGRAPHS BY DURSTON SAYLOR.

This residence is the home of the architects and their family. It was originally two separate
Colonial Revival structures purchased by them from the estate of industrialist Armand Hammer
in 2000 and renovated with appropriate period detail.

GIL P. SCHAFER III

HUDSON VALLEY FARM, 2007.
PHOTOGRAPH BY JONATHAN WALLEN.

JAMIE DRAKE

ENTRANCE HALL OF SUSAN WAGNER WING, SHOWING STAIRWAY TO BALLROOM,
GRACIE MANSION, NEW YORK CITY, DECORATED BY JAMIE DRAKE, 2002.
PHOTOGRAPH BY WILLIAM WALDRON.

WILLIAM DIAMOND
AND ANTHONY BARATTA

DICKSTEIN RESIDENCE, NEW YORK CITY, 1999.
PHOTOGRAPHS BY MELANIE DICKSTEIN.

JEFFREY BILHUBER

HAY FEVER, LOCUST VALLEY, NEW YORK, 2009.
PHOTOGRAPHS BY FRANÇOIS HALARD.

In 1935, more than a half century before Jeffrey Bilhuber renovated this seventeenth-century house, it had undergone a Colonial Revival renovation by antique collector and dealer Jane Robinson. Robinson had previously played a central role in the preservation and restoration of the late eighteenth-century building in Manhattan that had functioned as the Mount Vernon Hotel and later the Abigail Adams Smith Museum.

ADDIE POWELL AND NAN SWID

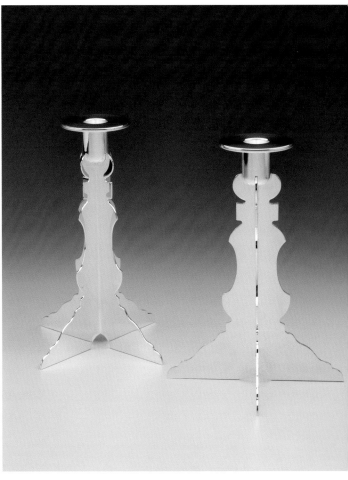

SILVER-PLATE PITCHER DESIGNED BY ROBERT A. M. STERN AND MANUFACTURED
BY SWID POWELL, 1986.

SILVER-PLATE CANDLESTICKS DESIGNED BY ROBERT VENTURI AND DENISE SCOTT BROWN
AND MANUFACTURED BY SWID POWELL, 1984.

JAMES BOYD AND ANNE REATH

POWDER ROOM WITH WALL TREATMENT BY BOYD REATH, TWIN FARMS INN,
BARNARD, VERMONT, JED JOHNSON ASSOCIATES, 1993.
PHOTOGRAPH BY JOHN M. HALL.

E. R. BUTLER

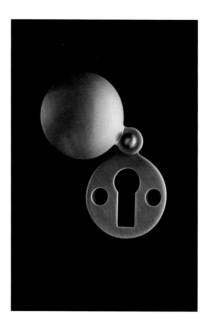

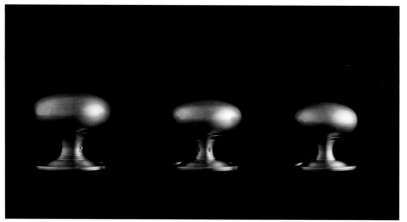

BRASS ARCHITECTURAL HARDWARE MANUFACTURED BY
E. R. BUTLER & COMPANY, 2010.

Of the numerous lines of architectural and furniture hardware produced by New York–based
E. R. Butler & Company, the W. C. Vaughan Company Collection, seen here, is especially relevant
to today's Colonial Revival. In business from 1902 to 2000, the Boston-based Vaughan firm
manufactured hardware derived from its vast archives of early-nineteenth-century patterns and
drawings. Houses in New England and the Atlantic seaboard were documented in the archive.
Among its many important clients, Vaughan provided hardware to the restoration of Colonial
Williamsburg in the 1930s.

TED MUEHLING

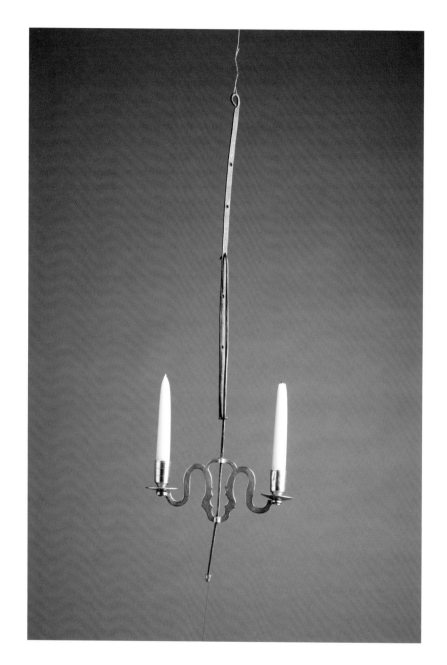

STENCIL HOUSE LIGHT FIXTURE, SHELBURNE MUSEUM, VERMONT, 1700S.

opposite

CHANDELIER PROTOTYPE DESIGNED BY TED MUEHLING AND INSPIRED BY STENCIL HOUSE
CHANDELIER, SHELBURNE MUSEUM, 2010.

NOTES

BIBLIOGRAPHIC NOTE

The bibliography on the Colonial Revival is extensive, and readers are encouraged to consult Dale Allen Gyure, *Colonial Revival in America: Annotated Bibliography* (Charlottsville: University of Virginia and Philadelphia: National Park Service, 2003). For this book we have found the following sources to be particularly valuable: Alan Axelrod, ed., *The Colonial Revival in America* (New York: W.W. Norton, 1985); Thomas Andrew Denenberg, *Wallace Nutting and the Invention of Old America* (New Haven and London: Yale University Press in association with the Wadsworth Atheneum Museum of Art, 2008); Briann G. Greenfield, *Out of the Attic, Inventing Antiques in Twentieth-Century New England* (Amherst and Boston: University of Massachusetts Press, 2009); Janet Kardon, *Revivals! Diverse Traditions, 1920-1945* (New York: Harry N. Abrams in association with the American Craft Museum, 1994); Karal Ann Marling, *George Washington Slept Here: Colonial Revivals and American Culture, 1876-1986* (Cambridge, Mass.: Harvard University Press, 1988); Max Page, *The Creative Destruction of Manhattan, 1900-1940* (Chicago: University of Chicago Press, 2000); William B. Rhoads, *The Colonial Revival* (New York: Garland, 1977); Elizabeth Stillinger, *The Antiquers* (New York: Alfred A. Knopf, 1980); Deborah Dependahl Waters, ed., *Elegant Plate* (New York: Museum of the City of New York, 2000), Richard Guy Wilson, *The Colonial Revival House* (New York: Harry N. Abrams, 2004); Richard Guy Wilson, Shaun Eyring, and Kenny Marotta, eds., *Re-creating the American Past: Essays on the Colonial Revival* (Charlottesville: University of Virginia Press, 2006).

WHAT IS COLONIAL REVIVAL?

1. While many Colonial Revival buildings, particularly in the East and Midwest, looked to Georgian inspiration, Southern California and Florida were influenced by the regions' Spanish heritage. Helen Hunt Jackson's 1884 novel *Ramona* mythologized the Spanish missions of the colonial era, sparking a widespread revival of architectural styles, but also launching an annual pageant, films, and a play. In 1887, three years after the publication of *Ramona*, the Hotel Ponce de Leon opened in St. Augustine, Florida, in a Spanish Renaissance style by the New York architects Carrere & Hastings. At the time of World War I, architect Addison Mizner working with sewing machine heir Paris Singer imagined a Mediterranean-style resort community in Palm Beach.

2. This and other aspects of the Colonial Revival are explored in Richard Guy Wilson, *The Colonial Revival House* (New York: Harry N. Abrams, 2004).

3. Wallace Nutting, quoted in Elizabeth Stillinger, *The Antiquers* (New York: Alfred A. Knopf, 1980), 190.

4. Henry Davis Sleeper, quoted in Samuel Chamberlain and Paul Hollister, *Beauport at Gloucester* (New York: Hastings House, 1951), 2.

5. "Old 76," *New York Mirror* 8 (March 19, 1831), 289, quoted in Barbaralee Diamonstein-Spielvogel, *The Landmarks of New York* (New York: Harry N. Abrams, 1988), 9.

6. Among the city's most ambitious Colonial Revival preservation efforts was the protection of a group of buildings on Staten Island that had previously been part of a community known as Richmondtown. Beginning in the 1930s, the complex, which in its assemblage evoked a small-scale version of concurrently preserved Williamsburg, was protected and made publicly accessible. For further discussion, see Landmarks Preservation Commission of the City of New York, designation report LP-0397 (August 26, 1969).

7. "A Style that Never Grows Old," *Popular Mechanics* 52 (November 1929): 279, quoted in David Gebhard, "The American Colonial Revival in the 1930s," *Winterthur Portfolio* 22 (Summer-Autumn, 1987): 109.

8. "The Union-square Building," *New York Times* (April 4, 1864).

9. Eleanor Roosevelt, quoted in "Bicentennial Seen as Help in Crisis," *New York Times* (March 22, 1932).

10. Ada Louise Huxtable's comment referring to an earlier proposal for the Susan Wagner Wing as a suburban garage appeared in Ada Louise Huxtable, "A Plan of Taste," *New York Times* (January 12, 1965). Subsequent quotations appear in Ada Louise Huxtable, "A Worthwhile Addition: Design for Wing at Gracie Mansion Overcomes Some Awkward Problems," *New York Times* (September 28, 1966).

11. Robert A. M. Stern, "Mott B. Schmidt and the Lost Generation of American Architects," introduction to Mark Alan Hewitt, *The Architecture of Mott. B. Schmidt* (New York: Rizzoli, 1991), ix.

A FLEXIBLE GRAMMAR

William Adams Delano, "Architecture Is an Art," *Architectural Forum* 72 (April, 1940):16.

1. "Architectural Criticism," *Architecture* 24 (October 15, 1911): 145.

2. "Royal Barry Wills," *Life* 21 (August 26, 1946): 67.

3. Christine G. H. Franck, *José M. Allegue: A Builder's Legacy* (privately published, 2002), 7.

4. "Town Hall to Open Drive in U.S. Today," *New York Times* (April 1, 1940).

5. Museum of the City of New York promotional material, c.1923, Gracie Mansion Papers, Museum of the City of New York.

6. William Adams Delano, quoted in Peter Pennoyer and Anne Walker, *The Architecture of Delano and Aldrich* (New York: W.W. Norton, 2003), 13, 100.

7. Text of capital campaign brochure as quoted in "Larchmont Temple: The Building's History." *Larchmonttemple.org*. n.p., n.d. Web. 10 Oct. 2010.

COLONIAL CHIC

1. Christopher Monkhouse, quoted in Laurel Graeber, "Genuine Imitations," *New York Times* (October 6, 1996). For an informative essay on Duncan Phyfe and Ernest Hagen, see Deborah Dependahl Waters, "Is It Phyfe?" in Luke Beckerdite, ed., *American Furniture* (Hanover, N.H.: Chipstone Foundation, 1996), 63–80.

2. Text of Erskine-Danforth Corporation advertisement, "Early American Furniture of true distinction, charm, and value," *New York Times* (October 16, 1921).

3. Facsimile of Warren McArthur sales booklet from the 1930s, produced by Nick and Shauna Brown, no date.

4. Augusta Owen Patterson, "When Ice Cubes Tinkle Against Silver," *Town and Country* (August 1, 1933).

5. Mary Ryan, quoted in Robert Schonfeld, "Marketing Easier Living," Donald Albrecht and Robert Schonfeld, eds. *Russel Wright: Creating American Lifestyle* (New York: Harry N. Abrams and Cooper-Hewitt, National Design Museum, Smithsonian Institution, 2001), 144.

6. American Modern Furniture catalogue, c.1935, quoted in Schonfeld, "Marketing Easier Living," 145.

COLONIAL BIBLES AND BALLYHOO

Eleanor Roosevelt, quoted in "Bicentennial Seen as Help in Crisis," *New York Times* (March 22, 1932).

1. Editorial, *Vanity Fair* (July 1926), 37.

2. Robert W. de Forest, quoted in Morrison H. Heckscher, Metropolitan Museum of Art, *A Walk through the American Wing* (New York: Metropolitan Museum of Art and New Haven: Yale University Press), vii.

3. R. T. Haines Halsey and Elizabeth Tower, *The Homes of Our Ancestors as Shown in the American Wing of the Metropolitan Museum of Art* (Garden City, N.Y.: Garden City Publishing Co., 1937): xxi-xxii.

4. "Old New York to Be Held Nov. 1," *New York Times* (October 24, 1926).

5. Walter Rendell Storey, *New York Times* (March 13, 1932).

6. Pearl Buck as quoted in America's Little House promotional material, 1934.

ACKNOWLEDGMENTS

This book has gained immeasurably from the help of numerous people in addition to those mentioned in the preface. We have benefited from conversations with the architects and designers featured in the book as well as from the efforts of students in a class we taught in spring 2009 in the MA Program in the History of Decorative Arts and Design at the Cooper-Hewitt, National Design Museum. We thank Elizabeth White, our editor at The Monacelli Press, for her scholarly advice and unflagging support. We also thank Rebecca McNamara at Monacelli and Lisa Delgado for their editorial contributions. Numerous people aided in getting images and the rights to reproduce them. The excellent new photography of artifacts was the work of John Halpern. In addition, we want to thank Connie Athas, Charles Burleigh, Margaret Caldwell, Suzanne Clary, John Stuart Gordon, Paul Gunther, Barry Harwood, Margaret Herman, Hänsel Hernandez-Navarro, Mark Alan Hewitt, Jeffrey Kroessler, Maggie Lidz, Richard L. Major III, Nancy Mandel, Earl Martin, Kory Rogers, Joshua Ruff, Ken Soehner, and James Tottis.

Donald Albrecht and Thomas Mellins

223

PHOTOGRAPHY SOURCES

© Peter Aaron/Esto 203; **Avery Architectural and Fine Arts Library, Columbia University** 45; 46; 47; 92; © **Bettmann/CORBIS** 32; 127; **Boyd Reath** 199; **The Brick Church** 101; **Brooklyn Museum** 119: Alfred T. and Caroline S. Zoebisch Fund (1993.156); 125: Bequest of H. Randolph Lever (64.80.22); **Carnegie Museum of Art, Pittsburgh, image** © **2006 Carnegie Museum of Art, Pittsburgh** 145: Purchase: Gift of Mrs. Louise Buck, Mrs. George H. Love and Mr. Warren McArthur (1999.11); **Photo** © **Christie's Images/The Bridgeman Art Library** 150; **Cooper-Hewitt, National Design Museum, Smithsonian Institution: Nancy McClelland archive, Wallcoverings** 23; 134; **Diamond Baratta Design, photographs by Melanie Acevedo** 210; 211; **K. A. Dombrowski-Sobel, kadsphoto. com** 28; 58; 59; **Drake Design Associates** 209; **E. R. Butler & Co., photographs by John Halpern** 31; 158; 159; 216; 217; **Fairfax & Sammons Architects, PC** 206; 207; **Fenimore Art Museum, Cooperstown, NY** 143 (bottom); **Ferguson & Shamamian Architects, LLP, photographs by John Halpern** 167; 174; **Girl Scouts of America** 181; **Gracie Mansion Conservancy** 33 (top); **François Halard/ trunkarchive.com** 212; 213; **Henry Street Settlement** 83; **Mark Alan Hewitt** 43; 64; **Hill-Stead Museum, Farmington, CT** 16 (bottom); **Historic New England** 18 (top); 132; 133; **Hoover Institution Archives, Stanford University** 187: Better Homes in America Collection (box 39, folder 1); **Jed Johnson Associates, Inc.** 215; **Collection of Juliette K. and Leonard S. Rakow Research Library of the Corning Museum of Glass, photographs courtesy Steuben** 164; 165; © **ChrisKendall.net** 202; **Larchmont Temple** 100; **Library of Congress, Prints and Photographs Division** 87; 98; 103; **The Long Island Museum of Art, History & Carriages** 27 (right); 80; **The Magazine ANTIQUES** 175; © **MASCA, courtesy of Manitoga/The Russel Wright Design Center** 156; © **Peter Mauss/ESTO** 41; 204; 205; **Memorial Library at the Boston Architectural College** 17 (top); **The Metropolitan Museum of Art, New York, NY, U.S.A., images** © **The Metropolitan Museum of Art/Art Resource, NY** 12: Gift of Mr. and Mrs. Franklin Chace, 1969 (69.194.1); 121; 122 (bottom): Gift of Lee McCanliss, 1961 (61.254); 148; 178; 179; **Ted Muehling, photograph by Loring McAlpin** 219; **Museum of Art, Rhode Island School of Design, Providence, Rhode Island, photography by Erik Gould** 116: Bequest of Commander William Davis Miller (59.253); **Museum of the City of New York** 42: Gift of Federal Works Agency, Work Projects Administration, Federal Art Project, 1943 (43.131.1.131); 85: The J. Clarence Davies Collection (29.100.2335); 143 (top): Bequest of Helen Van Praag Tallmadge (60.103.35); 161: Gift of Joseph H. Freedlander, architect of the Museum of the City of New York (33.50.1-.4a, b), photograph by Helga Studio; **Museum of the City of New York, Bequest of Percy L. Hance, photographs by John Halpern** 5: (75.156.17a); 6: (75.156.17b); 155: (75.156.18a, n, .21a); **Museum of the City of New York, Bequest of Percy L. Hance, photograph by John Parnell** 154: (75.156.17a-d, .18a, b, n, p, .19a, b, .20, .21a, b); **Museum of the City of New York, Gift of Mrs. Harry Horton Benkard (34.400.6), photographs by John Halpern** 122 (top); 123; **Museum of the City of New York, Gift of James C. Colgate (37.470), photographs by John Halpern** 3; 177; **Museum of the City of New York, Gift of Ms. Claire Lewis, photographs by John Halpern** 2: (91.102.1.5a, b); 4: (91.102.1.7); 115: (91.102.1.3); 153: (91.102.1.7); **Museum of the City of New York, Gift of Ms. Claire Lewis, photograph by John Parnell** 152: (91.102.1.1-.7); **Museum of the City of New York, Gift of McKim, Mead & White, 1945** 37: (90.44.1.288); 38: (90.44.1.1036); **Museum of the City of New York, Gottscho-Schleisner Collection** 29 (top): (88.1.1.750); 29 (bottom left): (88.1.1.752); 29 (bottom right): (88.1.1.758); 49: (88.1.1.1414); 50-51: (88.1.1.4481); 62: (88.1.1.1544); 63: (88.1.1.840); 68 (top): (88.1.1.3408); 73: (34.443.01); 74: (34.114.09); 75: (34.114.11); 84: (88.1.1.1861); 110 (bottom): (88.1.1.4984); 111: (88.1.1.4973); **Museum of the City of New York, Institutional Records** 77; 180 ; **Museum of the City of New York, photographs by John Halpern** 15: (44.242.1); 76: (34.191.1); 78; 79: Gift of Mr. Fordham W. Briggs, 1941 (41.523); 120: Gift of Mr. and Mrs. Benjamin Ginsberg and Messrs. Bernard and S. Dean Levy (86.172.3); 138: (56.375.2); 141 (bottom): (56.375.2); 147; 176: (34.505.22); **Museum of the City of New York, Wurts Brothers Collection** 26: (X2010.7.1.8562); 60: (X2010.7.1.8594); 61: (X2010.7.1.8089); 69; 91: (X2010.7.1.4568); 93: (X2010.7.1.7447); 95: (X2010.7.1.2878); 97: (X2010.7.1.12961); 105: (X2010.7.1.2369); 109; 194: (X2010.7.1.7650); **National Gallery of Art, Washington, DC** 191: (1943.8.4062); © **Genevieve Naylor/CORBIS** 197; **Collection of the Newark Museum** 124: Purchase 1989 The Members' Fund (89.87); **Collection of the New-York Historical Society** 44: (Negative #83754d); 117: (1950.298); 149: (Inv.14162); 162: (1939.476); 163: (1939.477); 182: (Negative #83715d); 192: (1939.271); 193 (top): (1939.177); 193 (bottom left): (1939.180); 193 (bottom right): (1939.183); **The New York Public Library, Astor, Lenox and Tilden Foundations** 66: Milstein Division of United States History, Local History & Genealogy; 82: Billy Rose Theatre Division; 88: Photography Collection, Miriam and Ira D. Wallach Division of Art, Prints and Photographs; 118: Picture Collection; **From The New York Times, March 13, 1932** © **1932 The New York Times. All rights reserved. Used by permission and protected by the Copyright Laws of the United States. The printing, copying, redistribution, or retransmission of this Content without express written permission is prohibited** 185; **New York University Archives, Photographic Collection** 99; **Al Nowak for On Location Studios/National Park Service** 128; 129; 130; 131; **Office for Metropolitan History** 104 (top); **David Paler Photography** 25; **The Pennsylvania State University, University Park, PA, Fay S. Lincoln Photograph Collection, Historical Collections and Labor Archives, Special Collections Library** 70; 71; **Copyright 1938 The Picture Collection Inc. Reprinted with permission. All rights reserved. Renderings courtesy Royal Barry Wills Associates** 55; **Platt Byard Dovell White** 86; **Pound Ridge Historical Society, photographs by John Halpern** 52; 53; **Private collection** 22; 27 (left); 30 (bottom, left and right); 67; 106; 110 (top); 112; 113; 136; 139; 141 (top); 142; 183; 188; 189; 195 (top); **Private collection, photographs by John Halpern** 21; 168; 169; 170; 171; 172; 173; **Queens Borough Public Library, Long Island Division** 68 (bottom): Postcard Collection; 81: Postcard Collection; 94: Frederick J. Weber Photographs; 96: Frederick J. Weber Photographs; 104 (bottom): Queens Chamber of Commerce Collection; 107: Postcard Collection; 108 (bottom): Postcard Collection; 140: Borough President of Queens Collection; 195 (bottom): Postcard Collection; **Queens Chamber of Commerce** 108 (top); © **Cervin Robinson, 2010** 10; 33 (bottom); 65; **Royal Barry Wills Associates** 56; 57; **Shelburne Museum** 135; 218; **Smithsonian Institution Libraries, Washington, DC** 146; © **Tiffany & Co. Archives 2010 Not to be published or reproduced without prior permission. No permission for commercial use will be granted except by written license agreement.** 151; **Unitarian Church of All Souls** 102; **Wadsworth Atheneum Museum of Art/Art Resource, NY**: 17 (bottom); 30 (top): American Decorative Arts Purchase Fund (1999.23.1); © **2010, Jonathan Wallen, www.jonathanwallen.com** 16 (top); 35; 36; 39; 89; 90; 208; **The Winterthur Library: Winterthur Archives** 18 (bottom); 19; 20; **Yale University Art Gallery** 137 (top): Gift of Francis P. Garvan, B.A., 1897 (1987.46.2); 137 (bottom): Gift of Francis P. Garvan, B.A., 1897 (1987.46.1a-c); 157 (top): Gift of Mr. and Mrs. William K. Wamelink (1987.60.1.1-2); 214 (left): Swid Powell Collection and Records, lent by Nan G. Swid (ILE2007.7.16); 214 (right): Bequest of Doris M. Brixey, by exchange (2001.11.1.1-.2).